KOALAS

KOALAS

AUSTRALIA'S ANCIENT ONES

TEXT AND PHOTOGRAPHS BY

KEN PHILLIPS

MACMILLAN • USA

MACMILLAN
A Prentice Hall Macmillan Company
15 Columbus Circle
New York, NY 10023

Library of Congress Cataloging-in-Publication Data

Phillips, Ken, 1947–
Koalas: Australia's ancient ones / Ken Phillips.
p.   cm
Includes bibliographical references and index.
ISBN 0-671-79777-8
1. Koala.   I. Title
QL737.M384P465   1994
599.2—DC20   94-14093
                                                    CIP

Designed by Irving Perkins Associates, Inc.

Manufactured in the United States of America

10 9 8 7 6 5 4 3 2 1

Page ii: *The world's most beloved marsupial spends the first six months in and out of its mother's pouch, and the second six months on its mother's back. Fathers play no role in raising joeys.*

To the patients of the Koala Hospital in Port Macquarie, New South Wales, operated
by the Koala Preservation Society of New South Wales, to
its founding members, Max and Jean Starr, May Laity,
to its many dedicated volunteers, and to Rod and Emily Cooper,
without whose knowledge, dedication, and friendship
this book would not have been possible.
To the memory of Jimmy Faison, who introduced the author to
his kindred spirit,
KOALA,
and to the late Jacqueline K. Ehrman, the author's mother, who
provided moral support for this project from the start.

Proceeds from the sale of this book will go to the Koala Hospital
and toward the care, rehabilitation, and preservation
of koalas and their habitat in Australia.
For further information contact the author, care of
Koala Preservation Society, P.O. Box 612, Cooper Station,
New York, NY 10276 USA

ACKNOWLEDGMENTS

Male koalas have a gland in the center of the chest which secretes an oily substance highly pungent with eucalyptus scent. They mark territory by rubbing against the base of a tree.

Thanks are due many people in many lands for their assistance, hospitality, and patience in helping the author express his love of koalas in a manner that he hopes does no injury to factual accuracy, historical detail, or the integrity or majesty of this early inhabitant of our planet. Deirdre Mullane, editor of this book, has the rare ability to hold tenaciously to superb editorial standards while at the same time allowing valued freedom in the creative process. Professor Paul Canfield, director of the School of Veterinary Pathology, University of Sydney, gave generously of his time, wisdom, and indefatigable good cheer and provided the author with the results of current research into matters of koala stress, disease, and physiology. Dr. John Fripp, at the Koala Hospital, Port Macquarie, contributed generously to the author's knowledge of this subject. Judy Dielman, the hospital supervisor, is a remarkable lady with a special connectedness to animals who instructs by doing. Robert Godbey provided his always sensible legal counsel and friendship. Bob Thompson was kind enough to share his koala archive in Sydney. Thanks also to my finest teacher, Terry Glen, a wonderful and loving koala seriously burned in a bushfire who trusted me to care for him and change his dressings every night, remaining a patient in the hospital for just over one year.

Many people gave generously of permissions to quote and abstract text and images. Thanks are due John Williamson and Matthews Music Pty., Ltd., for kind permission to reproduce "Goodbye Blinky Bill" © 1986 EMUSIC PTY., LTD., and "KOALA KOALA" © 1986 EMUSIC PTY., LTD.; The Australian Government Publishing Service for permission to quote and otherwise reproduce from "KOALAS—The Little Australians We'd All Hate to Lose." Reed Books Pty., Ltd., has been most generous in similarly permitting quoting and abstracting. *The Australian Geographic* was most helpful in granting permissions and referring the author to original graphic sources. I am indebted to Jay Hyams and Eleanor Gustafson whose reading and suggested changes to this manuscript have increased its readability and clarity. Any inaccuracies, serious omissions, or inadvertent representations are solely the fault of the author.

A NOTE ON THE ILLUSTRATIONS

THE PHOTOGRAPHS IN this book are the work of the author and are published here for the first time except where noted. The hand-drawn illustrations, charts, and maps are by Brad Johannsen, author of *High Tide*, *Occupied Spaces* and creator of numerous book covers, posters, and contemporary works. The reproduction on page 121, *Albert*, is an oil by Mr. Johannsen and is a caricature of Albert Einstein at the Institute for Advanced Study, Princeton University. Reproductions of the early anatomical drawing on pages 14–15 by Bauer are with the kind permission of the Library of the Natural History Museum of London. The photograph of Snowdrop (p. 3) was taken by Ron La Pla, Port Macquarie, New South Wales.

CONTENTS

Acknowledgments   vii

Preface   xii

THE BARE FACTS   2

The Marsupials   2

Why Koalas Are Found Only in Australia   21

Family Life   23

No Caviar Thank You!   27

Digestion   31

In Health and In Sickness   36

Until Death Do Us Part: Principal Causes   45

Sex and the Single Koala   49

Koala Psychology   60

FOR LOVE OF KOALAS   66

A Hospital Just for Koalas   66

Fire! The Story of Terry Glen   95

KOALAS, THE DREAMTIME, AND THE CREATION OF THE EARTH   116

Getting to Know Your Totemic Animal Spirit   133

WHAT THE FUTURE HOLDS   144

Bibliography   151

Index   153

When the last individual of
any race of living things
breathes no more,
Another heaven and
another earth must pass
before such a one
can be again.

WILLIAM BEEBE

PREFACE

As you journey through this book, you are invited—no, you are implored—to abandon your present view of the world and return to one we now know existed thousands of years ago, one that is being rediscovered not in the dusty anthropology departments of universities, but in high-energy physics laboratories around the world. This view reminds us that we must envision endangered species, including koalas, as living systems, not as superspecialized isolated outcomes of some evolutionary process based on "dominant" and "recessive" factors, but as integral parts of a network of living networks. Universal laws governing fundamental principles of change apply across and within orders of magnitude. Therefore, the principles of change underlying the behavior of a unicellular organism such as the paramecium are the same as those affecting a supranational organization such as the United Nations. Patterns of meaning that may be learned from studying and learning other forms of life are therefore pregnant with information having potentially universal applicability.

Such a realization or world view implies certain shared or codependent relationships between energy and matter, time and space, and all

Koalas are fussy eaters, eating only eucalyptus leaves and sniffing each one before munching.

that lives on this planet. In a series of lectures I presented several years ago, I demonstrated that the mathematical structure of the DNA molecule, which determines cytodifferentiation, the growth of cells into those of differing types and functions, was the same as the organizational structure of the I *Ching*, the ancient codification of universal laws of change, advanced by Taoist philosophers in ancient China. After I brought the audience, largely composed of behaviorial and social scientists, along to the point where the analogy became clear and obvious, their reaction, without exception, was one of amazement. This is highly symptomatic of the problem with our current world view. Had DNA been discovered several thousand years ago and the analogy with the I *Ching* made apparent to Lao-Tzu, I doubt if he would have been interested, as the universality of patterns of meaning *was assumed*. The same would be the case with Australia's native people, the Aborigines.

The process of getting back to the primordial, for those whose emotional and psychological roots are to be found there, is endless and constitutes a particular life style not suitable or practical for most people.

This is an ancient process characterized by many things: birth, dreaming, play, education, initiation, discovery of one's totemic or kindred spirits, celebration, creation. An important part of this process, for me, ironically, took place at the hands of Western civilization's most recent tool in a long history of expressions of man's search for artificial or divine intelligence: the computer. Having been something of a hacker long before most people knew what the word meant, I signed on to "The Source," one of the first public networks for owners of personal computers, of which there are now many. After a few moments, "Hi, TCE704, my name is Jimmy" flashed across the screen. The next two hours consisted of a digital conversation covering topics from Stravinsky to shamanism. Several weeks and a dozen or so computer sessions later, Jimmy said he sensed that I liked animals and that I should watch one of the morning news programs later that week. Not likely for me, as I am a night person, not given to either watching television or getting up at 6:00 A.M.

For some reason I did wake up and watch the show, a remote from Sydney, Australia, a part of the world I had not yet visited. Following several rather beautiful but uninteresting segments, the announcer promised that after a break the show would continue with live koalas and a "bush singer." What happened next is difficult to describe accurately, except to say that an awareness came over me when I saw the koalas that drew me very close to the television screen. Some chemistry kicked in, creating the feeling of having to see, touch, feel, and be with a koala, but there was a problem. "Goodbye, Blinky Bill," the song being sung by the well-known Australian bush singer John Williamson and a group of school children, was a tragic tale of the demise of the koala.

I soon realized that what I thought was a mythological product of my dreams was in fact one of the earth's oldest living creatures, the koala. I visited the wonderful land "Down Under" and discovered a remarkable couple who were caring for very sick koalas, night and day, in the specially converted basement of their home, and who with the help of dedicated volunteers and the local Rotary Club had built a small hospital to further their work.

Shortly after arriving in Australia, I learned the truth behind John Williamson's song, which is a tragic tale chronicling the destruction of one of the earth's most endearing yet misunderstood inhabitants. I was told that unless drastic measures were taken to protect the koala's habitat, they would nearly all be gone in a short time. This remains true today. Returning to New York I internally vowed to do whatever I could to help the koalas. My close friend of the computer networks—who had been a competition-winning concert pianist, award-winning photographer, and early pioneer in computer graphics software development—declined my offer of a trip to Australia and a few months later died, an early fatality of the disease later to be named AIDS. I was shell-shocked by the experience.

Today, the hospital is much larger, but not large enough, a wing having been added through the generosity of John Williamson, composer of the Blinky Bill song. A tree grows nearby honoring the memory of Jimmy Faison, who never made it to Australia.

The future of the koala is very unclear. Hopefully, this book is more than a collection of attractive images. Unless the word gets out to millions of people—who erroneously believe that Australia is covered with koalas—and unless their special eucalyptus trees are protected, this ancient, solitary, Earth Spirit who lives in the trees will go the way of the dodo and so many other extinct species and shall breathe no more.

It is incumbent upon us to therefore search deeply for the elements of implicate order, or what produces change out of chaos, and life-sustaining energy from entropy. To an increasing segment of our Western civilization, the realization that our long-held mechanistic world view is not working, that our approach to endangered species is inadequate, is becoming increasingly clear. This book invites you to go beyond these tantalizing philosophical points and play a role in preserving one of the earliest threads in the carpet of living beings on our planet.

It is also a warning. Should the koala be allowed to perish, it would be the end of the species of which the koala is the sole member. As more and more of the early stitches of the cosmic carpet cease to exist, the probability of the whole thing coming undone increases significantly. The koala's problem requires a "systems solution, with support from all over our planet."

KOALAS

THE BARE FACTS

THE MARSUPIALS

KOALAS MAY BE many things to many people, but one thing they are not is bears. There are no bears, or any animal remotely similar to a bear, in Australia. To call them koala bears is inaccurate and, if you have ever known a koala, something of an indignity! Koalas are what ancient cultures have come to recognize in myths as "tricksters." They may look cute and cuddly, hence the connection to the Teddy bear, but their cute looks are sometimes betrayed by their personalities, which may be as varied from one to the next as with humans. Most are quite independent, wanting little or nothing to do with adoring humans. They're generally not cuddly either, except under unusual and generally unhappy (as when they're sick) circumstances. Cuddling koalas can cause stress. While most people outside of Australia think that the country is heavily populated with koalas, most Australians have never seen one "in the flesh," except possibly in a zoo, which is not usually a good place for them.

As a marsupial, the koala belongs to a class of animals that is among the oldest inhabitants of our planet. Though many of the last members of several marsupial species perished long ago, we know that literally hundreds of forms once existed. Koalas go back over 50,000 years, in fact, to the period before the separation of the land masses into

Snowdrop, a rare albino koala. (Photograph by Ron la Pla, Port Macquarie, New South Wales.)

2

what we recognize today as the continents. So varied were the members of the marsupial species that even today the only trait they all have in common is their pouch. Even their pouches differ considerably as to the direction they face, size, teats, and so on.

When they think of marsupials, most people think of kangaroos, koalas, and if they are American, perhaps opossums. While most of these animals do have a *marsupium,* Latin for "purse" or "pouch," it is scientifically inaccurate to cite the pouch as the most differentiating characteristic of these unusual creatures. Several female marsupials do not have fully developed pouches, while several develop pouches only during their reproductive season. Most female marsupials, however, do have pouches, with the strongest and best developed ones belonging to those marsupials whose life style involves either a great deal of climbing—called phalangers—(such as koalas), hopping (such as kangaroos), or burrowing (such as bandicoots and wombats). Some entirely terrestrial marsupials have no pouches at all. Some pouches open to the front, as in kangaroos, while others are positioned so as to open toward the rear, as with wombats and koalas. The female marsupial's mammary glands are usually located along the abdomen, within the pouch, if there is one.

What differentiates marsupials from other mammals is actually their anatomy and physiology of reproduction. All marsupials lack a complete placenta—the semipermeable membrane that allows the transfer of nutrients from the mother to the developing embryo in the uterus. In marsupials, a yolk sack–like placenta is formed through which an outer membrane surrounding the embryo develops. Technically, this is known as an amnion. In only one group of marsupials, the bandicoots (*Marsupialia peramelidae*), is there a fully developed system more resembling that of placental animals.

Female marsupials have a duplicate reproductive system. For example, they have two vaginas spread sufficiently apart so as to allow the urinary tract to pass between them. When the birth process is under way, the offspring usually travel out via a third passage, the birth canal, which runs from the point of connection between the two uteri to the dual-purpose urogenital cavity. Interestingly, in many marsupials other than kangaroos, the median vagina is temporary and is reconstructed before each birth.

Tree of the Diprotodonta family, species having two front teeth. The koala is a single-member species among the marsupials.

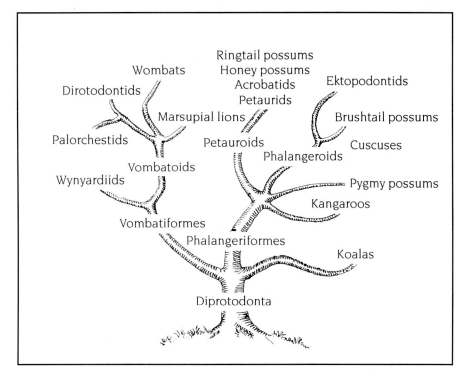

Male marsupials have an equally amazing reproductive system, at least when compared to most mammals. In many marsupials, the male, so as to be able to impregnate the dual vaginal canals of the female, has a dual-pronged, forked penis. The scrotum is also in front of the penis. The ducts that carry sperm from the testes run along the side of the penis parallel to the ureters, rather than in the center as is the case with placental animals.

Perhaps the most amazing aspect of reproduction in marsupials is the very short gestation period, 34 to 36 days, resulting in the birth of the young in nearly embryonic form. When "born," the undeveloped young, called a joey, a single offspring in the case of koalas, is smaller than the average human's shortest finger. It almost immediately begins a relatively long journey to the mother's pouch, in which it finds a nipple or teat to which it becomes attached. Indeed, the mother's teat extends quite far into the newborn and becomes engorged, assuring complete sealing and attachment. Details about the mechanism of migration, whereby the undeveloped fetus finds its way to the pouch, are unknown at present. The theory that the route was marked by saliva left by the mother licking the area was discounted as a result of observations reported in 1970. These observations noted that while the mother does lick the area, it is *after* the joey has passed by en route to the pouch. Presumably, this is done to clean the fur of any residual fluids left by the young.

Although the koala is not one of them, some marsupials, such as some kangaroos, have the ability to support and feed multiple offspring simultaneously in the pouch. Most impressive is the ability, again through a process not understood, to vary the make-up of mother's milk differentially for offspring at different stages of development. In this sense, the mother's pouch begins to resemble a modern gasoline service station in that "customers" may obtain higher or lower octane fuel!

Though the koalas from Victoria, New South Wales, and Queensland differ in appearance, the koala, whose Latin name is *Phrastolarctos*

"Koala" literally means "no drink." Leaves provide most of the koala's liquid requirement, but in a drought they have been known to drink water.

The koala's hand (left), with the significant two opposable thumbs, and hind foot (right). Note the length of the claws relative to digit length. The claws are crucial to the koala's ability to climb and to cling to a tree following a jump of up to ten feet.

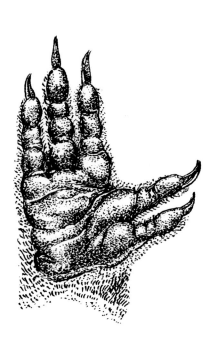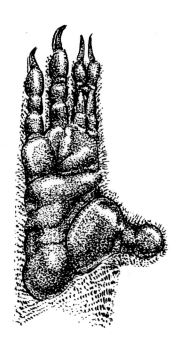

cinereas, is a single member species. The images and information provided throughout this book are generally of New South Wales koalas. Victoria, in Australia's south, is much colder in winter than Queensland or the areas in New South Wales where koalas live. Accordingly, koalas there tend to have longer, shaggier hair. Queensland koalas, compared with New South Wales members of the species, tend to be a bit smaller.

Koalas are nocturnal as are many of the marsupials. Their day typically begins when the sun is setting, in the late afternoon or early evening. By nature, koalas are highly arboreal, leading relatively peaceful, if solitary lives, high up in the eucalyptus trees. In fact, the koala has one of the most specialized diets of any living mammal; it feeds almost exclusively on the leaves of a small number of particular species of eucalyptus. Before the destruction of their habitat, koalas lived almost exclusively in their trees, being able to jump a considerable distance from tree to tree in their search for fresh, damp leaves. Almost all of their water intake comes from the leaves, often eaten while early morning dew is present. Eucalyptus leaves are efficient living storage systems for water; a full-grown tree can absorb several hundred gallons of water per day yet survive long and brutal periods of drought and even bushfires.

Koalas are extremely picky eaters, however, preferring only a few types of leaves at a time, from the relatively small number of eucalyptus species comprising their overall habitat. This fact has become particularly problematic in recent years as the destruction of their trees has been allowed to proceed at an alarming rate. There have been reports of koalas occasionally eating leaves from trees other than eucalyptus, such as the *Acacia costata*, *Bombax malabrica*, *Pinus radiata*, *Tristania conferta*, and *Tristania sauveolens*. To identify the eucalyptus trees that koalas universally

 **KOALA FOOD TREES**

Linean Name	English Name	Common	Less Common
E. *acmeniodes*	White Mahogany		•
E. *amplifolia*	Cabbage Gum		•
E. *blakelyi*	Blakely's Red Gum		•
E. *botryoides*	Southern or Bangalay Mahogany		•
E. *camaldulensis*	River Red Gum	•	
E. *camphora*	Broad-Leafed Sallee		•
E. *cambageana*	Coowarra Box		•
E. *cinerea*	Argyle Apple		•
E. *citriodora*	Lemon-Scented Gum		•
E. *creba*	Narrow-Leafed Red Ironbark		•
E. *dalrympleana*	Mountain Gum		•
E. *drepanophylla*	Queensland Grey Ironbark		•
E. *elata*	Willow Peppermint		•
E. *globulus*	Tasmanian Blue Gum	•	
E. *goniocalyx*	Long-Leafed Box	•	
E. *grandis*	Flooded Gum		•
E. *haemastoma*	Scribbly Gum		•
E. *largiflorens*	Black Box		•
E. *macrohyncha*	Red Stringybark		•

prefer with 100 percent accuracy is impossible, as information that has been recorded over the years from even within the relatively small number of areas where koalas continue to live has proven to be variable. A few species in each major region seem to be common such as the manna gum (*Eucalyptus viminalis*) and swamp gum (*Eucalyptus ovata*) in Victoria and the grey gum (*Eucalyptus punctata*) and red gum (*Eucalyptus camaidulensis*) in New South Wales and Queensland. Table 1 is based upon verified observations from within the Eucalyptus group.

Linean Name	English Name	Common	Less Common
E. *maculata*	Spotted Gum		•
E. *melliodora*	Yellow Box		•
E. *microcorys*	Yellow Wood		•
E. *nicholii*	Small-Leafed Peppermint		•
E. *obliqua*	Messmate		•
E. *ovata*	Swamp Gum	•	
E. *piluraris*	Blackbutt		•
E. *populnea*	Poplar Box		•
E. *propinqua*	Small Fruited Grey Gum		•
E. *punctata*	Grey Gum	•	
E. *resinefera*	Red Mahogany		•
E. *robusta*	Small or Swamp Mahogany		•
E. *rubida*	Candle Bark		•
E. *saligna*	Sydney Blue Gum		•
E. *scoparia*	Wallengara White		•
E. *sideroxylon rosea*	Pink Flowering Ironbark		•
E. *tereticornis*	Forest Red Gum	•	
E. *thozetiana*	Mountain Yapungah		•
E. *viminalis*	Manna or Ribbon Gum		•

Koalas are among the best-camouflaged marsupials, living high in the eucalyptus trees.

A great deal more misinformation is available about koalas than accurate data. In part, this is due to a genuine absence of scientific data. I was amazed at the lack of basic medical information pertaining to koalas when I first visited Australia many years ago. Far more was known about dogs, cattle, and other animals than this ancient ambassador. After living in Europe and the United States, where practically no information exists on the koala, I had assumed that I would find entire veterinary medical specialties devoted to the marsupials in Australia—such was not the case. This is beginning to change, however, and more research is being done on koala medicine and habitat matters now than at any other time in history. This is due in large measure to the fund-raising activities of the Australian Koala Foundation, the National Parks and Wildlife Service, and the practical experience gained from treating hundreds of koalas by the Koala Preservation Society of New South Wales.

The koala's principal predator has been human beings. One gains the impression that prior to the arrival of the Europeans, Australia was something of a "peaceable kingdom," as interspecies predation was relatively rare; koalas had few, if any, significant predators. It is possible but improbable that one of the carnivorous lizards, or goannas, might cross paths with a koala and attack, but the outcome of such an event would be uncertain.

The peaceable kingdom did not last, as shortly after the arrival of European settlers, the ease with which koalas could be caught became widely known. Literally millions of koalas were hunted and killed for their

THE BARE FACTS

Latin name:	*Phascolarctos cinereus* Koalas are marsupials, females having a pouch in which their young first develop. Their pouch faces the rear and has a drawstringlike muscle that the mother can tighten. They are the sole member of the family *Phascolarctidae*.
Subspecies:	There are three subspecies: *P.c. victor* (Victoria), *P.c. cinereus* (New South Wales), and *P.c. adustus* (Queensland).
Size:	Size is larger in the southern regions. Head-body length in the south averages 30.7 in./78cm for males and 28 in./72cm for females.
Weight:	Averages 26 lbs/11.8kg for southern males and 17.4 lbs./7.9kg for southern females. In the north, males average 14.3 lbs/6.5kg; females 11.2 lbs./5.1kg. At birth young weighs only .5 gm.
Principal predator:	Humans
Life span:	Their life-span today varies considerably due to stress factors, probably averaging 13–18 yrs.
Gestation period:	34–36 days.
Coat:	Thickest of the marsupials. Gray to tawny: white on the chin, chest, and forelimbs. Rump consists of tougher connective tissue dappled with white patches. Fluffy ears with longer white hairs. Coat is shorter and lighter in color toward northern regions.

First described in 1908 by E. Home.

magnificent fur. Poisoning and snaring became the preferred methods of killing, as shooting damaged the pelts. Records indicate that in the 1890s from 10,000 to 30,000 skins per year were being sent to London. By 1889 the volume reached 300,000! They were not used for high-fashion items but when a "cheap and durable fur" was required. By the beginning of the twentieth century, the koala populations of Victoria and South Australia were thought to be completely devastated. Counts in New South Wales were declining significantly. Queensland remained the only home to large numbers of koalas. Because of the fur trade, koalas finally became extinct in South Australia in the early 1930s but were introduced and are in Adelaide today. As early as 1898, legislation had been passed in Victoria that attempted to stem the killing, but such early efforts were largely ineffective and unenforced. In 1908, 57,933 koala pelts left Sydney harbor. At the time, little was known either about the highly specialized diet of koalas or the fact that koalas produce only one offspring per year, in contrast to other marsupials, which can be far more fecund.

One million koala skins were processed in Queensland following the declaration of open hunting seasons in 1915, 1917, and 1919. In 1921 the Queensland government, largely in response to public outcry, passed controls on the export of skins. This period of reprieve lasted only a few years, however. Massive unemployment and other economic conditions resulted in enormous pressure being placed on the Queensland government, which, in 1927, declared a one-month open season. The response was astonishing. Records show that licensing fees were accepted from just over 10,000 trappers. During the month of August 1927, 584,738 koalas and 1,014,632 possums of varying types were killed. Most of these pelts did not go to England, but rather to St. Louis, Missouri, in the United States. Groups in both the United States and Australia were outraged by the release of these numbers, which were probably low, as it was subsequently discovered that many "wombat" skins were, in fact, koalas. The export to the United States of koala fur masquerading as that of other animals was finally brought to an end when President Herbert Hoover, who had worked in the gold fields of Western Australia, signed an order permanently prohibiting the importation of both koala and wombat skins to the United States. That prohibition has remained in effect ever since.

By 1940, koalas were extinct in South Australia, only hundreds were left in New South Wales, thousands in Victoria, but tens of thousands in Queensland. Further reduction in populations was brought about by both disease and the clearing of land for government-funded road construction. Some wise Victorians in the 1800s translocated koalas to Philip Island and French Island; by 1923 the koala populations on these islands had outgrown the eucalyptus food supply, resulting in animals being brought back to sites where people thought they had once lived in previous decades. Today koalas live in Victoria, thanks to these early translocations by caring individuals.

The story of koala populations in New South Wales is more difficult to document. A survey of sorts carried out in 1949 indicated that the number had risen from the estimated 200 in 1939. In 1963 "several thousands" were reported to be living in New South Wales, according to Mr. Allen Strom, who was then the chief guardian of fauna for the state. In Queensland, data assembled in the 1960s indicated that koalas continued to live wherever suitable habitat was to be found, but much more recent satellite-imaging studies sponsored by the Australian Koala Foundation in Brisbane point to an alarming trend affecting habitat. Although Australia is one of the most urbanized countries in the world, with the vast majority of its population living in three very sophisticated metropolitan areas, it is estimated that by the year 2000, nearly two million people will live in what are now relatively undeveloped parts of Queensland, as well as the Gold Coast, which is already fully developed. This bodes badly for the koala, as its food trees are most plentiful in the coastal regions where there is the highest probability of development.

 **MORE KOALA FACTS**

- Koalas don't live in families, but are solitary animals.
- Koalas sleep as long as 18 hours a day and have a low-energy diet of eucalyptus leaves.
- Koalas are not "drunk" or otherwise intoxicated by their leaves.
- Although koalas obtain most of their water from leaves—the name *koala* is thought to mean "no drink" in several native Aboriginal tongues—they do occasionally drink water at the edges of streams.

Early paintings of koalas by the nineteenth-century Australian naturalist Ferdinand Bauer. They provided a glimpse of the anatomy and behavior of the koala. (Courtesy the Natural History Museum, London.)

Once again unemployment and economic recession are problems in Australia, as elsewhere, making the possibility of progressive environmental policy making at the cost of jobs slim, indeed. Stronger public policy is badly needed as legal loopholes permit continued exploitation of the koala in advertising and at theme parks. While "cuddling" koalas is now prohibited in some regions, this does not stop proprietors from opening venues where customers are charged admission fees to "pat" koalas. This is undoubtedly highly stressful for the animals; living conditions are also not likely to be well attended to by those who seek only to profit financially by harboring captive koalas.

One of the most significant differentiating characteristics of mammals is their ability to maintain a relatively constant body temperature, despite often drastic changes in the environment. The koalas, with their beautiful, thick fur, share this ability, having a body temperature of 36 degrees Centigrade, which averages about 2 degrees Centigrade below other marsupials. This lower body temperature is due to their lower rate of metabolism, which is also reflected in their sleeping up to 18 hours per day.

Koalas engage in a number of behaviors related to body temperature regulation, and the thickness and coloration of their fur plays a role of primary importance. On their backs and rumps, their coat is as thick as that of most Arctic inhabitants. Differences in coloration and marking among koalas are subtle, but nature has again expressed itself with great wisdom. Since koalas do not shed their coats in warm weather, they employ various methods to control body temperature. One of these is to make extensive use of the differing colors of their fur. Most of their bodies are covered with heat-absorbing dark gray fur, but their chests are pure white, except for the male's scent gland, about which we shall have more to say later. When outdoor temperatures are moderate, koalas are happy in the crooks of trees, quite oblivious to the rest of the world far below. In cold weather, common to winters in the south, koalas roll up into little furry balls when not grabbing at leaves to be eaten. In this manner, they conserve maximum heat, while still gaining thermal radiation as they sleep. In summertime, koalas reverse this process. Instead of rolling up into a round form, they lie back, leaning against one of the branches forming a crook in the tree. Both arms and legs dangle, leaving the koala's white chest exposed to summer breezes and bringing about maximum cooling. They often appear completely relaxed with their arms and legs dangling, and this summertime behavior is probably the origin of the widespread, but totally inaccurate, belief that they are drunk.

An observation that I have made several times, but which originated while treating burn patients in the intensive care units of the Koala Hospital in Port Macquarie, is that the koala's large nose, for which it is well known, is at times very warm to the touch, while at other times, and often only a few minutes later, it is very cool. (Now, if you ever have the opportunity to be in close proximity to a koala, *do not* attempt to touch its nose. This is a good way to get a very nasty bite and risk serious infection. I have at times built up a tremendous rapport with koala patients, even

The koala's low protein energy diet results in a requirement of as much as 12–18 hours of sleep per day. They are nocturnal, waking up as the sun sets.

The myth of the drunken koala is only folklore. There is no alcohol in the koala's diet of eucalyptus leaves. Humans observe koalas during daylight hours, which is the "middle of the night" for the basically nocturnal koala.

The koala's nose not only provides maximum surface area for nerve endings, but may play a role in controlling body temperature through internal evaporative cooling.

to the extent of rubbing noses, but this takes weeks, does not occur with most koalas, and is aided by a matrix of behaviors I present to the koalas.) This variation may be a further mechanism for regulating body temperature. Elephants, for example, can stem or encourage the flow of blood through the networks of capillaries throughout their large ears, which they flap in hot weather, lowering their body temperature.

A related observation, one that I have heard corroborated by organizers of African safaris, is that wild animals behave differently toward vegetarian humans than carnivorous humans. Supposedly this is due to the noticeably different body odor caused by the two varieties of diet. Eating a diet high in sources of uric acid, such as meat, seems to produce the odor characteristic of human "body odor." This is noticeably absent in humans who do not eat foods high in uric acid, though it requires several months to rid the system of these metabolites to the point where the odor is completely gone and undetectable by animals. It appears likely that animals such as koalas, with very keen senses, can detect this scent over great distances, and they may take it as indicating the presence of a predator.

In addition, koalas may reduce their body temperature in hot weather by increasing the rate of respiration. All the airway passages in the koala are moist, from the nostrils, which in the large-nosed koala also provide maximum exposure to surface area, to the windpipe. As a result, the koala can produce evaporative cooling in warm weather by breathing faster. When koalas do this, they must, however, conserve water. Here we have learned of another ingenious mechanism of the koala: the ability to alter the specific gravity and concentration of the urine. In hotter times, when greater amounts of water are needed for cooling, the urine is significantly more concentrated.

When the outside air is cold, koalas can slow down their breathing, and if this is not sufficient, they occasionally shiver; these fast contractions of muscle tissue generate considerable heat, given the koalas' slightly diminished body temperature.

Note, however, that both of these claims—that of capillary action in the koala's nose and that of a possible connection between a human's diet and the willingness of a koala to permit that human to get close— are based on my observations and *not* on systematic scientific research. They do, however, seem plausible.

KOALA PHYSIOLOGY

- Unlike bears or seals, koalas do not rely on a layer of fat below the skin as a form of insulation.
- Blood flow to extremities in cold weather, as in humans, can be reduced, resulting in the conservation of heat.
- Shivering has also been observed in cold climes as a means of creating heat through rapid contractions of certain muscles. This seems to occur when outdoor temperatures drop below 10 degrees Centigrade.
- When temperatures exceed 25–30 degrees Centigrade, koalas use evaporative cooling in their airways to regulate body temperature by increasing respiration rates. They can simultaneously reduce water loss by decreasing the amount of water in their urine.

WHY KOALAS ARE FOUND ONLY IN AUSTRALIA

THE CONCENTRATION OF marsupials in Australia and the fact that the island continent is the koala's only home has prompted significant debate and theorizing. Much of the fury has now subsided, with the theory of continental drift providing the best explanation, backed up by fossil and paleobotanical evidence.

Some 250 million years ago, our planet had a single supercontinent, referred to as Pangaea. This single mass broke into two large land masses: Laurasia to the north and Gondwanaland to the south. Several forms of animal life were already living on these land masses. Laurasia broke apart to form North America, Europe, and Asia; Gondwanaland split into pieces that today are referred to as New Zealand, Africa, and India; what are now known as Australia and South America were joined by a linkage that eventually became Antarctica.

It is important to remember that the formation of the ice caps at the earth's poles is a comparatively recent event. The earth was considerably warmer, with large areas of Gondwanaland covered with lush rain forests. Although conclusive evidence has not been found, it is thought that the earliest marsupials originated in the land mass that is now South America, and that they came across what was to become Antarctica, which was then heavily forested.

About 50 million years ago, the Antarctic land split, with a large piece, now Australia, drifting to the north. The marsupials were therefore "trapped" on this large mass of land, which was largely covered with lush foliage. As Australia continued to move northward, multiple climates started to evolve over different areas of the land mass. A wide variety of marsupials existed in the various climates and, not surprisingly, evolved into several different species. It is generally agreed that koalas first developed at this time. Fossil remains indicate that there were at least 12 different species of koalas that are now extinct. Today's koalas are therefore the sole remaining member of an entire family of koalalike animals.

Although koalas today are considered rather vulnerable creatures, it is clear that during some periods of their long history, they adapted to rather dramatic changes in their environment. For example, some 450 million years ago the polar ice caps began to form, as the Australian land

Habitat loss remains the largest threat to the continued existence of the koalas. The map at left shows area of koala food trees and populations in eastern Australia in 1800. The map at right shows the reduced territory in 1987. Significant further loss took place during the 1993 fires, most of which were thought to have been set by arsonists.

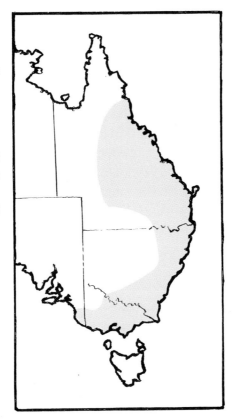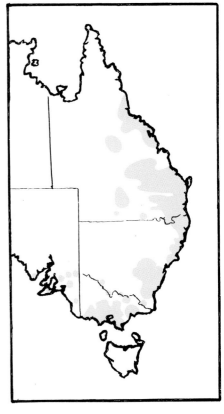

mass was pulling away from Antarctica. This presaged a significant cooling in the climate, which undoubtedly affected vegetation, and in all likelihood, changes in the koalas' diet. This period of cooling only concluded some 20,000 years ago. It is unclear whether the koala could survive such changes today.

Although the environment was quite different in South America and Antarctica millions of years ago, fossil evidence indicates that many early species of koalas were leaf eaters. The first koalas were inhabitants of rain forests, whose fossils have been dated at 14 million years old. Fossils from other koalalike species have been found in areas that were open forest areas, going back 4 to 5 million years.

The question of when the koala adopted its specialized eucalyptus diet cannot be answered through fossils, but botanists believe that the eucalyptus trees, of which there are now hundreds of varieties, became the principal food of koalas when Australia was largely covered with rain forests some 50 million years ago. This fact makes the koala one of the oldest living inhabitants of the earth. Although the koala has obviously adapted to climactic change, vegetative alterations, and geological shifts, it is the changes brought on by humans that so seriously threaten the koalas' future. Nonetheless, the species has remained steadfast in its attachment to the eucalyptus tree as its sole source of nutrition.

FAMILY LIFE

KOALAS ARE LONERS. Mating is a rather brief and infrequent event, producing only one joey at a time, usually once a year. Males are nomadic and play virtually no role in raising the young. The originally minuscule joey spends the first six months of its life in its mother's pouch. The second six months consist variously of living in the pouch and, as the joey grows, increasingly riding around on its mother "piggy-back" style.

Some mothers are more nurturing than others, but the sort of almost constant intimacy typical of some primates has never been seen on a sustained basis in koalas. Some mothers seem to be quite aloof toward their joeys, while others cuddle them and appear to take far greater interest. It is extremely important to remember that observations of animal behavior made in captivity may not be at all representative of behavior in the wild. In the hospital, we have observed that some mothers who are ill or seemingly debilitated may not care for their young. In such cases, and in the cases of joeys who have become orphaned because of automobiles having hit their mothers (an increasingly frequent tragedy as koala food trees become more scarce), we have infrequently but occasionally been able to place a joey with a surrogate mother, who will nurse it to maturity. Whether or not this works seems to have a great deal more to do with the personality of the mother than the joey.

This leads to an issue that has proven important and at the same time contentious: the content of the mother's milk. Much research is needed so that an optimum supplement can be arrived at. Several milk substitutes and dietary supplements are used at present in different facilities around Australia, but none is perfect. The further one looks into this question, the more complex the issue seems to become. Until unbiased research is undertaken by parties not likely to reap financial gain from the sale of the products involved, little may be said, except that the present protocol used at the Koala Hospital is adequate and works well. What has been observed clinically is that several components of koala milk, all part of or linked to sugars (or saccharides), seem to go

Except for brief mating encounters, koalas lead a solitary life.

A mother and joey peer out
at visitors.

Some mothers are more nurturing than others. Here a mother grooms her offspring.

through a three-stage process of change during the first year of the joey's life. Until more is known, the fundamental principle in medicine of not altering a treatment that is working should apply. The milk issue is not likely to be solved anytime soon. Always, when it comes to family life, even for this often misanthropic marsupial, "mother knows best!"

No Caviar Thank You!

No issue so clouds the koala's future as its highly specialized dietary requirements. Koalas are dependent on a very limited number of eucalyptus subspecies for their diet. The table on pp. 8–9 depicts those eaten by koalas in the mid-North Coast region of New South Wales, where the Koala Hospital in Port Macquarie is located. Although some entries on the list may change, the list is no longer in the few other areas where koalas remain. Not only do these trees thrive principally along the coast, which is prime land for plans of developers, but the koalas typically will not eat all types of eucalyptus all year long. Seasonal issues play a major role, but so do individual preferences, which seem to become more pronounced when the koalas are sick. These preferences may have much to do with the territory from which the individual animal came.

In this respect, running the Koala Hospital resembles a fine European hotel, as the dietary preferences must be noted and eventually logged in a computer database. Fresh leaves must be picked in accordance with these preferences and served within hours of picking, having been kept in cool water first.

Although koalas are nearly completely dependent on their eucalyptus leaves, they do swallow other things, including water and dirt. The former typically occurs in period of severe drought when the leaves are dehydrated and when heat prevents morning dew from forming. Ingestion of dirt is important for the operation of the koala's disproportionately large caecum, just one aspect of this marsupial's digestive system.

Properties of eucalyptus trees were observed by the earliest English settlers in Australia, not to mention their medicinal use by the Aborigines going back hundreds if not thousands of years. Hundreds of school children visit the Koala Preservation Society's Study Center each year for educational talks and presentations. Upon entering, many comment that the entire facility "smells like cough drops." The kids are perfectly correct. Not only do the leaves emit the unique aromatic scent, but the oil from the leaves is in part responsible for the koala's magnificent fur.

As far back as 1788, samples of eucalyptus oil were shipped out of New South Wales, and by 1852, an industry specializing in processing the oil was well under way. Thought originally to have a wide variety of medicinal applications, it was soon discovered that so-called essential oils based on terpinoids were anything but essential. In fact, most are extremely toxic to both humans and other animals. Some of the species favored by koalas are among the most toxic for other animals.

This realization led Australian biologists to question both the toxic effects on the koalas, as well as the animal's basic metabolic processes, given the near total dependence on a single, often toxic form of plant life. Aside from the 40 to 50 percent water content of the leaves (a full-sized eucalyptus tree can absorb hundreds of gallons of water a day), the koala's leaves contain little that would appeal to just about any other herbivore on earth.

All animal life as we know it requires proteins, fats, and carbohydrates. These three classes of nutrients are the fuel for metabolism and are essential for continued cellular reproduction within living systems. The typical human has a diet high (usually too high) in sugars and starches—both carbohydrates—ingredients that never amount to more than 10 percent of the koala's leaf diet. As a result of the absence of easily metabolized sources of energy, the koala leads a very relaxed existence, sleeping some 18 hours a day.

The ratio is reversed when the koala diet is compared to the human diet in terms of fiber. Human diets rarely exceed 10 percent fiber, while the eucalyptus leaves eaten by koalas often contain 30 to 50 percent fiber. Fiber is a very general term and refers to many things, most of which are difficult to digest and break down into usable sources of

The amount of water in the average eucalyptus leaf suitable for koala consumption varies depending upon rainfall.

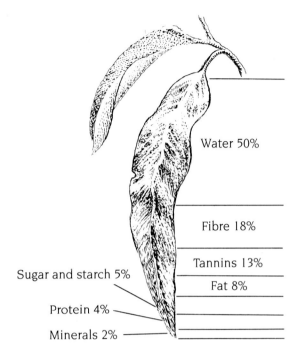

Water 50%

Fibre 18%

Tannins 13%

Fat 8%

Sugar and starch 5%

Protein 4%

Minerals 2%

energy. Nonetheless, it has very important biochemical and physical effects on the digestive system. Perhaps the nicest effect for those who care for koalas is the normal production of neat little pelletlike droppings that are easy to clean up! They are so compact that they do not dissolve easily in water—looking for droppings on the ground is one of the most efficient ways for locating koala territory in the bush.

Fiber has dual effects once in the digestive tract. While it absorbs water, it swells, sending signals causing animals to stop eating. In the case of the koala, which exists on a low-energy diet to begin with, fiber balance may be more critical. Humans, having large fat reserves as a rule, may suffer only minor side effects from temporary fiber imbalance, but koalas may become seriously debilitated, over time losing important resistance to disease.

Protein is continually broken down and resynthesized in animal life. The four bases of DNA compose a universal code that translates into amino acids, the building blocks of proteins. Patterns of proteins essentially determine the functions of every cell. For example, it is because the DNA-based information remains intact as cells duplicate that liver cells produce only liver cells and that chaos is kept to a minimum within living systems. Something of a mystery surrounds the ability of the koala to exist, even thrive, on a diet having as little as 5 percent protein—a protein level on which most other animals would starve.

The biological plot thickens at this point. Early settlers in Australia soon discovered that much of the export demand for the eucalyptus oil was coming not from medicinal applications, many of which were known to exist, but from tanneries in England. Word origins provide a clue here as *tannery* is derived of the same origin as the word *tannin*. Some 15 to 30 percent of the nonliquid content of the koala food trees consist of tannins, a group of compounds containing phenols, which increase the

While the koala's diet consists almost entirely of the leaves of a small number of eucalyptus species, they will occasionally ingest dirt, probably to aid the digestive process.

tensile strength and resistance of leather. Phenols accomplish this by bonding with the leather's proteins, fundamentally strengthening the leather. Within the digestive tract, tannins have essentially the same effect, linking up to proteins found in the diet, again already at a woefully low level in the koala in the first place. Additional bonding can take place with enzymes, as well as with carbohydrates. Consequently, the amazingly high level of tannins in the koala's diet could theoretically block the already minimal available proteins and even, under extreme circumstances, shut down digestion.

Interestingly, this doesn't happen in koalas because of the secondary effect of breaking down tannins: the release of phenols. Phenol is the active ingredient in many household disinfectants and cleansers and is the cause of the strong warnings against internal consumption of these products found on their labels! Quantities of phenols are seemingly absorbed by koalas with no ill effects. No wonder koalas are one of the cleanest animals on our planet!

DICESTION

No DISCUSSION OF the inner workings of the koala could be complete without mentioning its remarkable digestive tract. This is hardly a recent discovery, as it figures prominently in one of the more important ancient Aboriginal myths we shall look at later. Digestion is essentially the process whereby food is processed through a long chain of passages and storage points where it is broken down into molecular substances small enough or chemically simple enough to enter the bloodstream and be carried throughout the body.

Normally, koalas eat about a pound of leaves per day, though they actually require some five times that around to pick from. We have observed some animals eating a great deal more than this in the hospital, but this is probably due to their.having run out of food trees in their native habitat—an increasingly common problem as the habitat loses out to development. Koalas by no means eat all of the leaves they pick. Even on a single bough, they will be very fussy eaters, often sniffing each leaf and eating only the ones they like best, discarding the others. The process of scent detection is most likely a combination of behavior learned from the mother, genetics, and is possibly connected to the "pap" excreted by the mother and ingested by the young joey. The pap contains micro-organisms vital to the ability of the koala to digest its leaves. It functions much like the "starter mash" in wine making. It is a culture that introduces the essential gut fora. The preservation of these organisms presents a particularly paradoxical problem when it comes to identifying medications, particularly antibiotics, capable of ridding koalas of a couple of diseases that also threaten their long-term existence.

The koala has a set of 30 teeth well suited for its diet. As in the case of humans, koalas have four types of teeth: incisors, canines, premolars, and molars. The similarity ends there, as their size, shape, and placement are unique. At the very front of the mouth the koala has three pairs of incisors coming from the upper jaw. The first pair is sharp and chisel-shaped while the adjacent two pairs are more stumplike. Directly below them, from the lower jaw sit two large sharp incisors that project slightly outward and are curved as in an arc. They bear the full leverage of the powerful jaw muscles and are quite capable of inflicting a serious wound on a human hand! Moving toward the rear of the mouth a large space follows, filled only by a pair of small canines projecting from the upper jaw.

The gap ends at the premolars, of which there is a pair on each side. These teeth are important, as they are used to strip leaves off branches. When a koala finds leaves it favors, it may first use its front teeth to cut the branch off and then hold it with its hands, which are quite dexterous, placing the branch with leaves still on it sideways in the space between the front teeth and the premolars. The koala will then use the premolars to strip the leaves from the branch. Once the leaves are off of the branch, as in other animals, enzymes in the koala's saliva begin the breakdown of starches. The leaves are now moved toward the rear of the mouth, where they are ground by a repetitive action of the large molars, uniquely shaped for this purpose. I have made detailed video observations of this grinding process and have found that there is a little more to chewing than the typical human might think. The repetitive chewing patterns are not random. For example, any given koala may chew three times clockwise, followed by four times counterclockwise. The next koala may chew four times in one direction and four in another. The patterns seem to vary between animals, but not to any significant extent for any given koala. In addition, sometimes a koala will suddenly stop chewing, for no apparent reason.

Another curious ability the koala seems to have, reminiscent at least for North Americans of squirrels, is that of stashing a considerable amount of food in its cheek pouches. One day while cleaning out a yard and replacing leaves for Rio Rita, a patient now famous as the second koala known to make a complete recovery from an amputation due to gangrene, I noticed quite out of the blue that she started munching. No leaves had been in the yard for five minutes or so, indicating that she had stashed them away in her cheeks for some time! I mentioned this to another worker who said, "We frequently see a large male koala who makes a habit of storing leaves for later." This served to illustrate that those who have worked with animals for long periods of time, be they native indigenous peoples or those who have adopted the role in order to preserve endangered species, have absorbed vast amounts of knowledge not to be found in textbooks or scholarly journals.

From the mouth, ground food passes down the muscular tubelike esophagus. The muscles along this pipe contract in a wavelike manner assisting the food along in its journey to the stomach. The koala's stomach is surprisingly small: about the size of a baseball. At this point, the breakdown of starch is well under way. Sugar and protein breakdown begins as acids and enzymes are brought into play in the stomach. It is also thought that most of the absorption of the eucalyptus oil takes place at this point.

After processing in the stomach, food travels into the ileum, which is equivalent to the small intestine in a larger animal. Here lipids or fatty acids are broken down. Protein continues to be reduced here as well. The small intestine plays a major role in first-stage nutrition entering the bloodstream.

Following preliminary processing in the ileum, the largely still undigested food moves on to the most remarkable component of the koala's digestive tract, which is part of the "hind gut." The hind gut consists of several sections: the colon, the caecum, and the rectum. As in many other animals, the colon consists of two major segments, as opposed to three in humans, for example. The end of the colon most near the small intestine is quite enlarged, even bulbous. Protruding from the junction between the colon and small intestine is yet another structure, which is the koala's greatest cause for notoriety among naturalists and zoologists: its caecum.

This amazing structure is often 200 cm or more long, and 10 cm in diameter. Many people notice that the koala seems to have a perpetual "pot belly." This is due in large measure to the size of this close-ended tube that inflates even more after feeding. (Awareness of the amazing structure central to the koala's ability to survive almost entirely on its eucalyptus leaves forms the basis for the Aboriginal myth explaining the origin of the rainbow, which we shall explore later.) W. C. Mackensie, one of the most respected of the early Australian anatomists, declared the koala to be one of the most advanced of all mammals. Andrew Pratt,

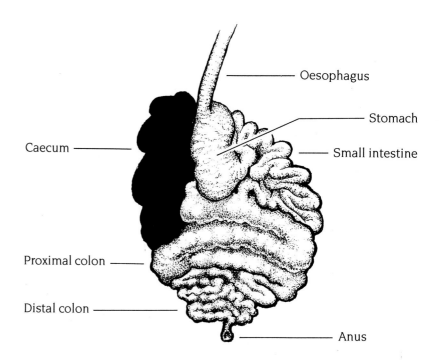

The koala's digestive tract, with its disproportionately large caecum.

writing in his well-known early volume *The Call of the Koala*, stated that the process whereby the koala may forge growth of its own muscle, bone, and blood components must be most advanced and mysterious. Indeed, at first blush, the size, efficiency, and operations of the koala's caecum do seem to pose a problem for the advocates of the early models of evolutionary theory. This is no longer such a puzzlement, however, for although we do not know exactly why the koala is so biologically "locked on" to the eucalyptus, we now know that separate systems within a given species are quite capable of developing independently, given sufficient time.

Study of the koala's caecum revealed a process of great importance to many creatures that came into being much later: symbiosis. Although there still are many unanswered questions concerning the operation of the koala's caecum, the first revelation was that enzymes produced by the koala's own digestive system are definitely inadequate for the high fiber content, mostly cellulose, of their leaves. Indeed, in many mammals, including humans, a flora of micro-organisms coexist quite happily within the digestive tract. Nowhere is this process more crucial than in the koala's caecum. There micro-organisms feed upon and break down carbohydrates. As research over the years has shown, micro-organisms are essential to the digestion of all plant-eating animals, though not all have caecums. In many animals, either the micro-organisms function directly in the stomach or, as with cows, for example, there may be multiple stomachs with the contents shifted from "tank to tank," essentially functioning as a living refinery. In the process they take what they need, generally a very small quantity or "overhead factor" of proteins, leaving the rest for the host organism to absorb. Sometimes the micro-organisms can actually convert formerly indigestible compounds into vitamins.

Some anatomists cite the appendix found in humans as a vestigial remain of some sort of caecum, which might have been at one time more developed and active under different dietary conditions. Speculation on the function of the koala's caecum has also focused on a secondary function as a water-storage facility. I have observed that koalas occasionally eat dirt. This would lead one to question whether, as in some other animals that also eat dirt and have an active caecum, the particles in the dirt, along with peristalsis (the process whereby intestinal contents are moved along), are used to "grind" undigested food. Such additional functions of the caecum are, for the most part, yet to be confirmed.

What is known is that the lower end of the colon is an enormously efficient extractor of water from the digestive contents. This is also crucial for the koala, which must endure the effects of long periods of drought and, at times, a very limited water supply. In this sense, the koala is enormously efficient. Similarly, the koala has such a low metabolic rate that it consumes about 50 percent less oxygen than other animals of the same weight. While a casual observer might attribute this to its relaxed life style, this is a case of cause and effect reversal—the lower metabolic rate actually dictates this life style, which over the years has served the koala well. In addition, of course, it has earned the koala the well-deserved reputation among naturalists as having one of the most advanced digestive systems on the planet.

In Health and In Sickness

It is impossible to trace the long-term history of diseases in koalas because no historical records exist, except those taken from the Koala Hospital since 1973. That the origins of the Koala Hospital in Port Macquarie first began with volunteers caring for koalas in their homes makes their early, detailed record-keeping effort even more impressive. These records, covering thousands of cases, will provide an invaluable database for future research, but they were entered manually on case cards and then placed in storage. It is just now, as this book goes to print, that the Koala Preservation Society of New South Wales, Inc., which operates the Koala Hospital and Study Center, is computerizing these records.

Our insight into illnesses affecting koalas is therefore based upon information collected fairly recently. This is good, in that the protocols followed, forensic data, and population statistics are of good quality as far as they go. This state of affairs is far from ideal, however, because it is not possible to draw many firm historical conclusions of a highly scientific nature using the standard statistical methods students suffer to master in graduate school. This picture may change as the records in Port Macquarie become computer accessible, but obviously that data will describe only koalas in the Hastings region. As we shall see, there is reason to believe that habitat destruction, urbanization, external stress factors, environmental dynamics, as well as more traditional issues of infectious diseases, play significant roles in the overall question of koala health. There are, and no doubt have been for hundreds of years, significant variations in some of these factors from region to region. This is particularly true in comparing the North Coast of New South Wales and Queensland with Victoria, where koalas were once plentiful in a significantly colder climate.

Before looking at specific illnesses, a few observations might be of use. First something of a paradox: The koala is no newcomer to the planet, and although fossil evidence suggests that several forms of the animal have disappeared, the species has adapted to several changes, including a remarkable degree of domestic encroachment by human civilization, resulting in the destruction of over 70 percent of the koala's habitat. This would, in theory, indicate a robust, resilient creature. Yet it appears that koalas and their ability to resist disease can be severely compromised by stress. The issue, of course, is what constitutes the causes of stress and at what point does it become a contributing factor to illness. Basically, we don't know.

My observations and the even more substantial experience of the founders and workers at the Koala Hospital have directed the spotlight on a few likely culprits. While virtually all of these issues are in one way or another related to human beings, some are more controllable and avoidable than others. It is important to stress again that koalas are wild animals. Being high arboreals, they normally have no human contact whatsoever. They live in the tops of trees. (The eucalyptus trees in Australia, by the way, are a good deal taller than those on the West Coast of the United States, for example.) Captivity of nearly any kind seems to cause stress in some koalas and disruption of complex forms of behavior, such as mating. Although an enormous national parklike facility would probably benefit koalas, given the proper planting of koala food trees, confinement in smaller facilities of any kind can produce serious stress. The life expectancy of koalas in zoos is significantly less than in "free roaming" koalas.

To determine a koala's age, examination of the teeth is still the best index, when carried out by an experienced volunteer or researcher. Indeed, we have seen some "old" koalas who have become debilitated because their teeth have worn down to a point where they can no longer adequately cut and chew their leaves.

Koalas with injured jaws at the Koala Hospital are provided with a diet consisting partially at least of pulverized leaves and a dietary supplement, as needed. The koala's particular selection of favorite eucalyptus leaves are first cut up into strips with scissors and then placed in a blender, along with water and other dietary supplements or medication, as needed. The resulting green liquid is a soda-fountain delight few koalas resist, except when very ill.

If a koala is observed sitting on the ground in the woods, this is taken as a most ominous sign of severe stress or illness. Sadly, according to those who have put in the most number of years at the hospital, out of thousands of patients, no one could recall one case of a koala found curled up on the ground making a successful recovery. The Aborigines have for thousands of years believed that all animals played an important role in the Dreamtime, when the earth was created, and that as spiritual beings, the animals know when their time has come. There is probably great truth in this, at least on the biological level, as koalas seem to come down and sit on the ground before dying. It is highly unlikely that when koalas die they just fall out of the trees.

The destruction of habitat and of "corridors" between habitat pockets is likely to add significant stress and certainly danger to a koala's life. As mentioned earlier, koalas require a variety of eucalyptus leaves, though their overall number is low. Although koalas can jump several feet from tree to tree, the habitat has thinned or disappeared altogether in some areas, so there are now often no trees to which to jump.

At dusk, when koalas awake, one can often observe them marching on the ground, looking for a food tree. Sometimes they must travel

Hairline fractures of the jaw are common injuries to koalas hit by speeding cars. Weeks may be required before the injured animals are again able to chew leaves. At the koala hospital, a pulverized "soft diet" is provided, along with nutrients.

considerable distances to find one. Since the forests were destroyed and roadways cut through, not only have most of the trees been eliminated, but access to those remaining has been prevented. Risk of being hit even on local roads is high because, being nocturnal, the koalas have poor eyesight when they are confronted with bright light, such as the headlights of a car. In addition, the color of their gray fur is not in significant contrast to that of the tarmac. In a rural land, where distances tend to be great, cars also tend to be moving at high speeds—often too high to stop for a dazed animal in the road.

Though koalas might be able to cross a country lane, this is not at all the case for the expanding network of highways serving the magnificent rural areas and coast line of Australia. Even on local sealed roads, koalas are frequently killed. One of the most heartbreaking aspects of working at the hospital is when travelers call to report finding a dead koala on the road. Koalas are a protected species, and people who either encounter an injured koala or inadvertently hit one on the road should report the incident. Some people may be reluctant to become involved in

While road signs may help prevent some koala-car collisions, motorists pay little more attention to these than to any other cautionary sign.

The principal threat to koalas is the destruction of their habitat by man. Here a young koala in desperation has taken refuge in a house being constructed where his home once stood.

summoning help for fear of involvement with authorities, paperwork, or legal proceedings. The fear is unfounded but widespread.

Roadways often cut through corridors, or routes that koalas have been traversing for thousands of years. Developers, town councils, and others have been implored not to permit the interruption of these critical life lines for koalas. This is accomplished with varying degrees of success. We frequently receive calls at the hospital for a koala "out on the road." When the rescue team responds, they often find a debilitated animal quite dazed, often walking around in circles, completely disoriented and showing definite signs of stress. The increased frequency of these calls during the traditional mating season tends to indicate that territorial disputes may be playing a role as well, but this, too, is made worse by the lack of trees brought on by human commercial development.

Abrupt, loud noise frightens koalas and produces heightened tension that probably leads to chronic stress over time. The abruptness of the noise is important. Koala caregivers in Australia know about a colony of koalas in Queensland that stayed put even when a large air force base

Although a koala could defend itself against an attacking dog with its claws and strong arms, its instinctual repertoire prevents this from happening. Dog attacks are now a major problem where koalas and human civilization intersect.

was constructed nearby. The colony seems to have adapted over time to the loud fighter planes taking off and landing. This, however, appears to be the exception rather than the rule. At the hospital, great care is taken to keep noise levels low—even to the point of using sliding doors rather than hinged ones, which can slam, disturbing the koalas.

The visual signs of stress vary somewhat, depending upon cause and situation. Animals brought in from road accidents, dog attacks, being trapped in construction sites, and similar misadventures often appear dazed, their eyes protruding with a seemingly fixated point of focus. These animals should be considered dangerous and are likely to bite and scratch. Specific training and absolute care must be exercised in

The most rewarding days are those when patients are released, fully recovered, back into their original territories. Canvas bags, which the koalas seem to like, are used for transport.

their rescue and subsequent immediate treatment. Respiration rate is often elevated and may remain so for several hours following such an event.

When koalas are transported from an accident scene and when they are released back into the wild following recovery, they are placed in large canvas bags with ventilation holes. Carried gently, they seem to like this treatment and become calm, at least until taken out of the bag. I have, on more than one occasion, sat in a car with an injured koala sitting in a bag on my lap. The motion and soft vibration of the moving car seem to have a calming effect.

Recent research confirming early observations might lead one to believe that the koala may be physically less able to cope with stress than other animals. The scope of our discussion of stress here does not permit detailed coverage of the physiology of stress, but the ability of animals to cope with the effects of stress is determined to a large extent by a number of substances produced in the adrenal glands.

Surprisingly, as far back as 1924, Will Mayo, one of the founding brothers of the famous Mayo Clinic, indicated in public lectures that the koala had inadequate adrenal glands and that there was a high degree of probability that its diet of eucalyptus leaves was providing some compensatory substance. More recent research indicates that this is not so, but the basic observation that koalas have among the smallest adrenals relative to the body weight and size is correct. Only the wombat has a similarly undersized adrenal, perhaps adding support to the assertion that the wombat is the koala's closest biological relative.

With the issue of stress as possibly the determining factor for prognosis, along with the general physical condition of the koala, we can break down the major areas of disease into the following categories. In addition to trauma and physical injury, these are the most frequent causes of death in koalas: diseases of the urinary system, respiratory disorders, digestive-system pathologies, multisystem disease, and tumorous (neoplastic) disease.

A number of other illnesses are often seen but are not always lethal. In fact, koala research has in recent years considerably improved the outlook if conditions are detected and treatment provided in time: "wasting," pneumonia, diseases of the eye (conjunctivitis and keratitis), nonfatal cystitis, topical skin growths, parasitic infections, and mange.

With his ears healed this same patient is now nearly ready for release. Traumatic stress is as much a concern as physical recovery.

UNTIL DEATH DO US PART: PRINCIPAL CAUSES

WHILE PRESENTING NUMBERS can be a risky affair, Professor Paul Canfield, director of veterinary pathology at the University of Sydney and a fellow patron of the Koala Hospital, recently published a particularly valuable set of figures comparing the number and percentage of koalas that died from causes we have just listed. Shown in the following table, these numbers are for an overall population of only 207 koalas from the Port Macquarie area. I know of no other similar statistics from other regions, which would make any analysis of variance between regions possible. In addition, these numbers are based on a small sample, by standard statistical criteria. Nonetheless, these findings are of potentially great importance.

PRINCIPAL CAUSES
OF DEATH IN NEW SOUTH WALES KOALAS

Finding	N(koalas)			
	In the Wild		Captive	
	Number (%)		Number (%)	
Trauma	62	(38)	2	(4)
Urinary Tract	34	(21)	5	(11)
Multisystem Disease	20	(12)	7	(16)
No Detectable Lesions	15	(9)	11	(24)
Respiratory	11	(7)	6	(13)
Tumors	11	(7)	4	(9)
Miscellaneous	6	(4)	0	
Digestive System	3	(2)	10	(23)
TOTALS	N=162		45	

Clearly among koalas not in captivity, trauma, mostly by automobile, is the primary killer of koalas. This in turn is caused by the destruction of the koalas' habitat at the hands of human beings. At one-half this level is the most frequently encountered disease-related cause, urinary tract problems. Obviously, protection of habitat, which requires no expensive medical research, would lower or eliminate the most frequent cause of death.

Urogential issues, the most frequent cause of death other than physical trauma, are often found along with problems in other organ systems. The most frequently seen problem is generically called cystitis, often referred to as "wet bottom," and seems to afflict males and females with equal frequency. An afflicted koala has little appetite, is dehydrated, debilitated, and often shows signs of muscle wasting if the case is advanced. They are also typically listless, depressed, and unresponsive.

The principal cause of this set of problems has long been thought to be a form of chlamydia, fortunately not a form easily transmitted to humans. Chlamydia is actually a large family of many dozens of forms of bacteria. Antibodies indicating exposure to chlamydia in the cases of both free-ranging and captive koalas has been confirmed. Kidney problems are sometimes found in koalas with signs of cystitis or wet bottom, but there are also cases of kidney dysfunction without any signs of wet bottom.

Another relatively frequently encountered problem is conjunctivitis, which shows up either alone or sometimes along with respiratory disease. Happily, even progressed cases of koalas with granulated tissue conjunctivitis respond to antibiotic ointments. In the 1970s *Chlamydia psittaci* was identified as a causative agent in conjunctivitis. There is no way of knowing how many koalas lose their eyesight while living in their natural habitat, since this problem is usually detected only secondary to some other circumstance that has brought them to the hospital. Unfortunately, the koalas don't know to seek treatment at the hospital when their eyes become infected—though some koala patients have returned to the hospital seeking human contact entirely on their own!

Pneumonia has also been found in koalas. There is evidence that the forms of pneumonia frequently found often begin as opportunistic infections, again raising the question of why and how the koalas' ability to ward off these pathogens has been compromised. We have no clear answer at present. In all likelihood, a combination of factors is at work. Since these data are from autopsies, it is unclear whether recent bouts of pneumonia are the norm for these animals, or alternatively, a long history of debilitation precedes succumbing to an opportunistic case of pneumonia.

Disorders of the koala's unique digestive system, at least based on Professor Canfield's statistics, reveal an interesting trend: They are essentially ten times more frequent in captive animals than in those that are free roaming. Again, the numbers are so small in the sample that this statement must be reduced to the observation that this kind of problem is, for some reason, seen in captive koalas more frequently than in free-roaming animals. This seemingly significant difference may be due to any number of causes: human manipulation of diet (including the use of various milk substitutes, dietary supplements), tapeworm, reduced exercise while in captivity, and others. Much more research is needed as a wide variety of gastrointestinal problems has been found upon autopsy; but without historical evidence, "cause" is impossible to identify with any certainty.

Often koalas present problems affecting many organ systems. For example, many suffer simultaneously from conjunctivitis and cystitis. Kidney problems are sometimes seen in cases also involving septicemia, the invasion of the bloodstream by micro-organisms from the site of an infection. Patterns of multiorgan diseases are notoriously difficult to diagnose and pinpoint the causes of in any species. In the case of the koala, with the significant absence of long-term historical data, this problem, for the time being, appears insurmountable. Perhaps as records are assembled into computer-accessible formats, patterns will emerge. Additional funds are needed to purchase the equipment necessary to conduct this sort of research.

All that may be said about the issue of multisystem disease at this point is that it may be due to susceptibility to a common entity or group of organisms (such as *Chlamydia psittaci*), serial disorders that set in after a single illness or repeat single illness weakens a koala, or specific patterns brought on by particular organs becoming dysfunctional.

Some of the seemingly organ-based illnesses may in fact be secondary to trauma. Some researchers have, for example, observed seemingly inchoate forms of cystitis following treatments for other, sometimes less complex, problems, such as a broken bone. Perhaps the change of environment or the koala's first experience with humans may produce reduced resistance, allowing problems that may have existed at a subclinical level to suddenly come to the forefront. Again, we are a very long way from understanding these patterns in koalas. For these reasons, human contact with patients at the Koala Hospital is minimized and an environment as close as possible to the koala's natural space is maintained.

Although much effort is being focused on diseases responsible for significant reductions in the koala population, as Professor Canfield has pointed out, loss of habitat and widespread ignorance of the koalas plight are in the long run just as serious.

CHLAMYDIA: A COMMON DISEASE

Chlamydia is actually a large family of bacteria that is dependent on host cells for its continued existence and growth. The chlamydia are actually quite primitive and cannot synthesize high-energy compounds on their own. Energy-rich substances are provided the chlamydia by the host cell they infect.

Two forms of chlamydia are most common: *Chlamydia trachomatis*, which is a leading cause of preventable blindness in humans, causing trachoma, and *Chlamydia psittaci*, which is common in birds and, as we have seen, plays a significant role in a variety of problems afflicting koalas. Birds have been identified as the vector responsible for transmitting psittacosis to humans.

Conjunctivitis has been known to exist in koalas for over a century. *Chlamydia psittaci* has been isolated from the eyes of large numbers of koalas in the wild, as well as hospitalized animals—both those showing symptoms and those not. Evidence supports the hypothesis that chlamydial infection can produce infertility in the female koala.

SEX AND THE SINGLE KOALA

KOALAS ARE SURELY one of the earth's most beautiful and endearing inhabitants, but sexy they're not! By now, perhaps, you are beginning to see an emerging pattern. Koalas are different from other animals in many respects. Sex is no different. I know of no other mammal in which courting is initiated and carried out by the female, rather than the male.

Although courting is begun by the female, during the mating season, which reaches its peak by October and is generally past by December, the mature male makes a very loud bellowing call. Upon waking at dusk, the male points his nose straight up in the air, inhales deeply, making a sound somewhat like a snore, and then, in an act of diaphragmatic breathing that would put the finest opera singer to shame, suddenly exhales, making a sharp belchlike sound. He then inhales again, repeating the whole process. The noise is stunning.

During the mating season, mature males, waking at dusk, point their heads up and produce their impressive bellow.

On my first visit to Australia, never having heard this noise before, I was quite startled and couldn't imagine what sort of wild beast was lurking in the night around the grounds of the motel in which I was staying. The sounds resembled those a wild boar might make, not an innocuous-looking koala! These calls can carry far distances and have the effect of causing other males to start calling as well. When several koalas are bellowing in close proximity to one another the sound is

Each patient at the koala hospital receives an ear tag, on the right ear for females, left for males. Tag numbers are linked to computerized case files for research and readmission use.

A calling koala. During breeding season, and occasionally at other times, koalas will adopt this position and produce a deep, loud, guttural sound which in the quiet of the forest may be heard for long distances.

JANUARY
Peak mating period
Peak birth period
Lactating
Young in pouch
Independence

FEBRUARY
Some late mating
Peak birth period
Lactating
Young in pouch
Independence

MARCH
Some late mating
Some late births
Lactating
Young in pouch

APRIL
Some late births
Lactating
Young in pouch

MAY
Lactating
Young in pouch

JUNE
Lactating
Young in pouch

JULY
Pap production
Pap feeding

AUGUST
Bellowing, fighting
Pap production
Pap feeding

SEPTEMBER
Bellowing, fighting
Emerge from pouch

OCTOBER
Bellowing, fighting
Emerge from pouch

NOVEMBER
Peak mating period
Peak birth period
Lactating
Young in pouch
Emerge from pouch

DECEMBER
Peak mating period
Peak birth period
Lactating
Young in pouch
Emerge from pouch
Independence

Calendar of events in the koala life cycle.

Koalas may love to sleep; however, they do so more because of their low-energy diet. Their bottoms are padded with connective tissue for comfort.

deafening. Bellowing normally begins at the age of three and becomes most frequent in koalas four and five years of age.

Koalas exhibit little group or hierarchical behavior of any significant complexity. Socially complex behavior is hardly dictated by a daily life style characterized by 14.5 hours of sleep, 5 hours of munching, and the rest of the day pleasantly relaxing in the crook of a tree or climbing around in search of a more comfortable venue. They are completely self-sufficient to the extent that they neither burrow, construct nests, or even rearrange any component of their environment to their liking. Even in

This hungry male was clearly photographed outside of the breeding season since the sternal gland is not discharging heavily.

inclement weather, koalas rarely seek shelter of any kind. Unless it is particularly cold, they will move further out on limbs during rain, receiving the full force of the elements. The koala's fur is not only thick, but extremely oily. These two factors provide the koala with perfect weather proofing; it is unlikely that cold or dampness even penetrates the depths of its coat. If it is cold when rain falls, koalas curl up in a furry ball to conserve heat rather than to remain dry.

While complex behavior outside of mating seems not to exist in koalas, they are territorial. They have a very sensitive sense of smell that is used for both reading subtle differences in the types of eucalyptus they are considering eating and in detecting territorial boundaries. The male koalas have a scent gland located in the upper center of their chest, where the sternum would be felt. During the breeding season this gland secretes a highly viscous and smelly substance used for marking trees. It is a highly concentrated, musky eucalyptus odor that, at least up close, most humans find unpleasant. Since the oily substance discolors the fur immediately surrounding the gland, the resulting mark is, perhaps, the easiest way to determine the sex of a koala from a distance. Territorial marking with the scent gland is frequently coupled with calling, sometimes after fighting with another male, infrequent attempts at mating, and after being released or handled by humans.

Territorial marking takes place at the bottom of the tree. The koala will sometimes stand at the bottom of the tree and rub his chest against the trunk. When he is climbing particularly thick tree trunks, however, the gland is rubbed along the bark simply as a matter of climbing. The marking behavior seems to begin in males as young as the eighteenth month and becomes most frequent at the age of four or five, roughly paralleling the peak of sexual behavior.

Within the largest recovery yards at the Koala Hospital, I have observed koalas marking over where another had previously placed his mark. While this indicates lack of any reluctance to invade another's territory, the value of this observation must be questioned, since this behavior occurs in captivity, where over the years hundreds of koalas have lived. No attempt is made to "wash down" or otherwise remove the scents from the trees. Similarly, it is thought to be extremely unlikely that any of the most frequently encountered serious diseases are communicated through the scent gland residue. The available literature contains a

Typical koala postures (from upper right):
Sleeping in the crook of a eucalyptus tree in warmer weather; resting while moving between trees on the ground; mother and joey in the crook of a tree; eating a bunch of leaves; limbs dangle while sleeping; sleeping in crook of a eucalyptus tree during cooler weather; (upper center) active koala climbing by starlight. A lone koala distressed for lack of a food tree. For thousands of years, when eucalyptus forests were plentiful, koalas rarely ventured on the ground in search of food.

Shortly after release this koala began territory marking by rubbing his sternal gland against the base of his new home.

few accounts of females engaging in scent-gland marking even though, of course, they have no such gland. (I have thus far never observed this behavior.)

As noted, the most unique sexual tradition carried on by the single koala is that it is the only mammal in which the female does the courting. Foreplay is elaborate and can be rough. The captive female appears to be in heat for only a few hours, less than a complete day, at a time. While in heat, the female goes through a series of patterned behaviors, which might not by the inexperienced observer necessarily be directly associated with sex. The process appears to sometimes be set off by the presence of a male or the sound of his bellowing. The female, while holding on to her tree, will begin a subtle but frequent jerking motion. With every so many little jerks, she will flap her ears. While in heat, she will in fact go and visit males and in the foreplay stage engage in behavior which appears to emulate male behavior at other times. The female may attempt to mount the male. I have seen females put their arms on a male's shoulder and begin by giving little nips or bites to the male's neck. The male sometimes feigns disinterest but at other times may bite back, creating the appearance of a violent fight. The male may open his mouth wide and make threatening sounds, while the female may make a strange growling sound back at him. The seduction may take some time, at least 15 minutes, and create quite a tumult. If one is not aware that this is foreplay, the wildness of the behavior could easily have one worried about the plight of the "loser" of such a battle, which, of course, is no battle at all.

Intercourse and copulation for koalas is a quick affair, lasting perhaps a couple of minutes at the most. Clearly far more fun is had during the foreplay stages. The male will eventually mount the female while both are in a vertical position in their tree. The male will then give the female a series of short nips on the neck, open his mouth wide, and grab a hold of the back of her neck. The female elevates her hind parts while the male penetrates. This does not take very long. The female appears to experience an orgasmic sequence of contractions after the male has withdrawn and throws her head back several times.

The female then wishes to be free of the male and makes a squeaky call, signaling her annoyance. Often the male will not decouple immediately and offers the female one more love nip on the neck, at which point the female, having had quite enough, may attack the male vigorously, to be rid of him.

It is noteworthy that sometimes males will attempt to mount a female not in heat. Though they usually meet with reduced resistance after nipping the female's neck and because the female is not in heat, she does not raise her rump, making intercourse impossible. It is difficult to say whether these are spontaneous whims of the male, or whether perhaps some more subtle cueing system is at work. Penile erections are common in males, even juveniles, and can be brought on by aggressive play or even bellowing of other koalas.

Not only is the female courting behavior unique to koalas, but neck biting typically occurs only in serious predatory forms of behavior or among cats as a means of carrying the young, which koalas do not do. Since the koala is not a predator and does not carry its young in its mouth, the use of neck biting seems out of place. The female's role is particularly aggressive in the sex life of koalas; however, given that nonsexual aggressive behavior can produce arousal in the male, such a predominate style of mating may be required for the process to unfold.

The above observations were made of koalas in captivity at the Koala Hospital and are based upon detailed reviews of videotapes made of koala behavior. The sex life of koalas is bound to be somewhat different in the wild, where the literature reports significantly longer heats, lasting sometimes several days. Several "old wives' tales" surround the sex life of koalas: that they have clusters of females following them, that they have harems, that they pay "prenuptial visits." Like the notion that they are drunk from alcohol in their leaves, there is no truth to any of these tales. Dominant male territories may include several females' trees, creating the impression that some sort of collection of females is taking place. There is no evidence, however, to support a selectively patterned group of females for any one male.

KOALA PSYCHOLOGY

BONDING BETWEEN JOEYS and mothers is close, but not unique. That is, the joeys do not seem to react uniquely to their mothers. On the other hand, my attempts to introduce an orphaned joey to a stuffed, surrogate mother koala were successful for only a short period of time, indicating such techniques could not reasonably be expected to meet with success. Joeys seem willing to accept milk and cuddles from any female but the reverse seems not to be the case. Only a minority of females will "adopt" joeys, though there seems to be variance in the degree to which females will perform the role of mother. A mother without a joey on her back can occasionally be seen roaming around as if looking for her baby. In such a

Koalas have definite yet often subtle personalities. As is the case with their markings, no two are alike.

state, the mother seemingly will respond to squeaks made by any joey. Similarly, if any joey who is evidencing this behavior is placed on a mother's back, she will seem quite satisfied without knowing whether or not the young one is hers.

Male koalas play no role in the rearing of the young. Koalas are essentially fatherless, psychologically speaking, as the biological father is out of the picture minutes after mating. Unlike kangaroos, koalas never "box," or even strike with their paws and very sharp nails. This in a sense has not served them well since the arrival in Australia of Caucasians, who brought their pets, particularly dogs, with them.

At about the age of ten months, the offspring begin to explore the world without the aid of the mother koala. At first these jaunts are short in both distance and time but quickly increase. The young appear to be indecisive about taking leave of the mother's back, where they hitch a ride. Sometimes the joey will become fascinated with playing in dirt or eating. Should its mother leave while this fascination persists, the young one can become quite upset.

At the age of about ten months, joeys start to explore the world without their mothers. Shortly thereafter, they are no longer welcome on Mom's back.

Joeys will play games with others, their mothers, and even attempt to trick humans by feigning sleep.

Play behavior is often very revealing, and although I have seen entries in koala literature suggesting that koalas do not play, this is certainly not the case with the young. Within the recovery yards of the Koala Hospital I have observed young koalas playing games of "hide and seek," for periods of up to ten minutes. They will also scrap with each other in a playful manner to varying extents. They will selectively play with their caregivers; however, typically and not surprisingly, they are much more apt to do so in the middle of the night—usually about 11 P.M. Within a group of younger koalas, under two and a half years, I have seen temporarily "neglected" young become jealous of another receiving human attention.

Mature koalas appear at times to experience dreaming. I have observed rapid eye movements in patients of the Koala Hospital, along with abrupt involuntary muscle contractions coupled with grunts and facial expressions surrounding the mouth.

Perhaps more surprising, elements of primitive "tooling" behavior have been observed among young playful koalas while very active late at night. While one of the young, Pebbles, was being given formula and

63

Koalas will spontaneously stop and contemplate a route to a desired limb or other goal.

leaves late at night inside the hospital, her two yard mates attempted to climb up a clothes rack that had inadvertently been left next to the building, so that they could observe what was going on inside. After climbing up on the rack, they realized that it was not positioned well. They jumped off the rack, attempted to move it, and again climbed up on the small plastic rack. While they achieved their wish of watching the proceedings, they, of course, were unaware that if they both went to the same end of the clothes rack, their combined weight would cause it to fall over, which is exactly what happened. The surprise collapse of the wash rack sent them scurrying up a nearby tree, where they continued to watch, until Pebbles and I returned to the yard, when they resumed playing. While I was tempted to buy them various toys and observe their behavior further, such fascinating and admittedly enjoyable pursuits would teach the koalas that humans are playful and to be socialized with, which in the long run could be a deadly mistake. Once released back into the wild, they might well seek out humans and encounter less than friendly ones, their pets, and their children. The ability to formulate patterns of simple tooling behavior indicates that koalas are possessed of greater intelligence than early observers, who were probably deceived by their lassitude, reported.

Although young koalas seem to vary between tolerating and craving human contact, without exception, they reach a point, also early in their lives, if left alone, when they almost automatically withdraw to the trees, not coming down even to look at a human with whom a former bond had been formed. Yet as patients, once they recover from whatever trauma brought them to the hospital and adjust to their initial contact with the human race and its odd ways, they exhibit astonishingly trusting and co-operative behavior during treatment.

Within the limits of their basically sedentary life style, individual koalas as observed on the grounds of the Koala Hospital have distinct personalities. The vast majority are without doubt best described as aloof. At both extremes, however, are koalas that are grumpy and truculent, on the one hand, and gregarious and dependent, on the other. While there are few behavioral differences that may be applied across the board to differentiate between the sexes, other than mating behavior, I feel that the males are often more affectionate and vulnerable, while the females can be more protective, aloof, and defensive.

FOR LOVE OF KOALAS

A HOSPITAL JUST FOR KOALAS

Most koala patients are surprisingly trusting of their human caregivers.

WHAT IS WITHOUT doubt one of the most singular institutions in the world began in 1972 in the small town of Port Macquarie in rural Australia. While the plight of the koala had not been a happy one, even back then, an extremely farsighted couple, Jean and Max Starr, local shopkeepers, organized what was to eventually become the Koala Preservation Society of New South Wales—perhaps the most progressive group devoted to saving Australia's most beautiful ambassador to the world. The original focus of the organization, which remains central to its mission today, was the preservation of the habitat so critical to the future of the koala, education, and co-ordination of activities with smaller groups in other parts of the country. The Starrs originally had no idea of whether the town, which had a population of only around 10,000 at that time, would support such an effort. Most townspeople either had no idea that koalas were in the area or took their existence for granted. With enormous assistance from the owner of the local newspaper, Mr. Charles

Uptin, and one of the early National Parks and Wildlife Service officers, a public meeting was held. The encouraging response on that day in March 1973 was to lead to the establishment of a remarkably dedicated group working under license from the National Parks and Wildlife Service.

At first, not surprisingly, a major problem was that no one knew exactly which leaves composed the koala's diet. A list had been obtained but turned out to be of species eaten in mountainous Victoria—quite useless information for a group seeking to establish an effort in coastal New South Wales. One of the first efforts, therefore, was to establish a koala observation team that would observe from which trees the koalas were eating. By now, it was realized that weather, altitude, soil, and climate govern the types of eucalyptus trees that grow in specific areas; the local koalas had adapted to these tree types. These leaves were then identified by a forestry official, leading to the formation of the list used today.

Tree planting was the first major effort of the society. When the first shipment of 100 eucalyptus trees arrived, the early members of the society wondered how they would ever plant all those trees. In practically no time at all, over 12,000 trees had been planted. No sooner had they been planted than they became delicious food for local wallabies; obviously, more had to be known about koalas, their trees, and the feeding activities of other species in the region.

Every year, hundreds of sick and injured koalas are treated at the Koala Hospital by volunteers who respond to emergency rescue calls 24 hours a day.

A co-operative local council enabled the society, with the assistance of the local Rotary, Lions, and Van clubs, to plant larger areas such as the water supply catchment area. Tree corridors were planted following creeks and linking up the larger parks, thus allowing the koalas to disperse safely. Mr. Uptin's *Port Macquarie News* ran a column approximately every two weeks called "Koala Corner," informing local residents of the latest adventures—and misadventures—of the society and koalas. There is no doubt that the Starrs' efforts would not have prevailed without tremendous local support.

In the first year, three koalas were cared for. The first had conjunctivitis. For five weeks, the members tried to catch the first patient, who by then had been called Pop Eye. To this day, all patients of the society are given names by those who first encounter them. Human names are off limits. Usually the name is somehow related to the circumstance or locale from which the koala came, for example, "Blaze" from a fire, "Aquatic" from a river or swimming pool, or "Rafters" from an attic or roof.

By the time the society finally caught up with its first patient, it was totally blind, the disease having spread to both eyes. The society did what it thought was the correct thing at the time and built an enclosure for the koala. The enclosure was small by today's practices, but little was known of the relationship of stress to the course of illness. Researchers from the town of Armidale visited Pop Eye. Doctors Alan Jackson and Frank Cockram took cultures from the animal and concluded that some sort of bacteria was involved. These researchers were later to establish that the disease was chlamydia and that it could affect and debilitate koalas in many ways, for example, conjunctivitis, pneumonia, and wet bottom syndrome. Because so little was then actually known about the diseases affecting koalas, Pop Eye soon died, striking a discouraging but not fatal blow to the morale of the early members. The second patient, Cubby, was a beautiful young female koala found in the gutter covered with ticks and suffering a partial paralysis. Being the first young koala reared by the group, she did not have a large tree to climb in while growing up, and as the day of her planned release came closer, there was much anxiety that she wouldn't know what do to when placed at the bottom of a large tree. The fears were unfounded, as she scurried right up a huge eucalyptus. Her calls could be heard at night for some time to

Caregiver/patient assignments are rotated to prevent overbonding. Should koalas become too attached to humans during treatment, they might seek them out after release.

come. She produced magnificent joeys every year for several years and became a source of great pride and encouragement. While Cubby was being reared, another patient, a young male joey, Tiny Tim, came into the hands of the society. Tiny Tim wasn't strong enough to hold on to his mother, as is customary for about six months after a joey has permanently emerged from the pouch. Tiny Tim, never a strong animal, remained near the Starrs' home and within earshot of the society members' voices to which he had grown accustomed. He lived until about the age of seven.

At this point, record keeping was started, as the diversity of koalas and their varied plights became apparent. About two dozen animals were treated in 1974, when the record keeping began in earnest. By 1990, over

2,000 treatment records existed. In 1975, it became apparent that the society needed some sort of place where the koalas could rehabilitate. The Port Macquarie Apex Club, a service club for people under 40, built the first little Koala Hospital in the Macquarie Nature Reserve (it still exists today), and two recovery yards were provided at that time, but many animals were still cared for at home.

Leaf collecting became more difficult as the number of koalas being treated grew. Going out each morning often before dawn, Max Starr collected leaves for years. As the existence of the society became more known, it had to be careful not to become an object of political leverage by private interests. Those who wished not to have a road built or other easements granted might attempt to cite the effect on the koalas or other environmental issues, right or wrong, as part of efforts to protect their own objectives.

A second hospital was built in 1986 near Roto House, a beautiful original Australian home now used by the New South Wales National Parks and Wildlife Service as its local headquarters. The trees around Roto House and the hospital even to this day are home for many koalas and possums. In these early days, the Koala Society ran several raffles as a means of obtaining financial support. The *Port Macquarie News* also ran a local appeal for funds, which provided initial funding.

Often joeys must be hand-fed, but human hands must not touch the leaves!

The Roto House, a restored home, is now regional headquarters for the National Parks and Wildlife Service, adjacent to the Koala Hospital.

The third stage of development came a few years ago with the construction of the John Williamson Wing. One day, John Williamson, an Australian country music singer, happened to be in Port Macquarie and decided to visit the Roto House and Koala Hospital. While he was visiting, an emergency rescue call came in, and the famous visitor found himself suddenly abandoned. The entire experience so impressed John that it inspired him to write "Goodbye, Blinky Bill," predicting the loss of the koala. The song became enormously popular throughout Australia. John very generously donated earnings from the song, often placed in a hat passed at performances, long an important Australian tradition at such affairs, to the Koala Preservation Society. When the song was recorded, proceeds from that effort were generously donated as well.

Although the koala is now a protected species, meaning that it may no longer be hunted or kept as a "pet" in captivity, the Koala Preservation Society of New South Wales receives no financial support from either the federal or state governments in Australia and is entirely dependent on its dedicated roster of volunteers, local merchants, and tourists, who drop coins in a donation box. Sadly, the society has no endowment and essentially lives hand to mouth. Despite the fiscal uncertainty over its future, the Koala Hospital, which operates as one of several society functions, continues to provide state-of-the-art care for its koala patients.

A DAY IN THE LIFE OF A KOALA HOSPITAL PATIENT

Patients at the Koala Hospital are cared for in one of three places. If an injury or illness is neither life threatening nor dangerously contagious to other koalas, a sick koala might be in one of the recovery yards out of doors. These facilities look normal enough, but their appearance belies an enormous amount of planning and forethought. Some of the yards are quite large; several are not. All have koala food trees in a variety of sizes so that the environment may meet the exercise needs of both large and small patients. It is important for koalas to continue to exercise while recovering in order to prevent deterioration of muscle tone. The yards are

Patients unable to climb trees rehabilitate in sheltered "gunyahs" in the hospital's many yards.

arranged in such a way that the koalas cannot use the trees to jump into adjacent yards or to leave the hospital altogether.

A patient may be placed in a yard with "gunyahs," small shelters under which the main trunk of a tree has been placed so that you may walk along it on all fours. The horizontal runner is usually three to five feet above ground and is supported by two metal pipes, one at each end. To these supports, which also hold up the small roof (the sides of the gunyahs are completely open), are attached two-foot plastic canisters into which boughs of leaves are placed. The containers are then filled with water to keep the leaves fresh.

A koala with a far more serious condition would be placed alone in an intensive care unit. The intensive care units are in the John William-son Wing of the hospital, where additional leafing facilities are located as well as a treatment room equipped with all emergency materials, an incubator, and high-intensity lighting for more delicate treatments. Minor surgical procedures are sometimes carried out here. Major surgical procedures, usually involving the orthopedic and ophthalmic areas, are carried out in town, where the chief of veterinary medicine has surgical suites equipped with movable X-ray and anesthesia machines. A few local physicians have demonstrated their humanity and dedication by assisting with operations on koalas, contributing both state-of-the-art equipment and medical knowledge. Such has been the case leading to development of protocols where amputation is required due to gangrenous infection, when cataract formation has become serious, and in treating koalas rescued from forest fires. If an infant or joey requires around-the-clock feeding and temperature control, it might end up at home with a fully trained member of the Koala Hospital staff, as the society is licensed to provide this type of service.

At approximately 5:00 A.M. each day, "leaf pickers," trained in the botanical skills of identifying the leaves of appropriate Eucalypt species, set out in a specially outfitted vehicle to collect the day's supply of leaves for patient meals. The special leaf picking truck, donated by the National Parks and Wildlife Foundation and the Sun Herald Koala Fund, has an overhead platform on which the pickers stand. They have a standard compliment of leaves to pick each day, augmented by special instructions left by the hospital supervisor the evening before, based on any new admissions. Clipping what amounts to a good-size truckload of

Koalas severely stressed or injured can require a private room in the Intensive Care Unit. Noise, temperature, and light are carefully controlled.

One of two blind patients eagerly awaits dietary supplements from a volunteer. Blind koalas appear to form cognitive maps of their environs quickly.

leaves on a daily basis is not easy, particularly as there are fewer and fewer available trees nearby. The process involves tough work, often beginning at dawn in difficult weather. Sometimes patients come from considerable distances, making the task of matching their leaf diets even more complicated.

When the "leafing" is completed, boughs are brought back to the hospital, sorted by type, and placed in large buckets of cold water that in turn sit in special sinklike tubs. Some patients require more specialized diets, such as only "young" leaves, and separate receptacles exist for these within the leafing room. Young joeys or koalas recovering from hairline fractures to the jaw may require easier-to-chew leaves.

Between 6:00 A.M. and 7:00 A.M. the first crew of volunteer workers, along with a shift supervisor or hospital supervisor, arrive. First, the night log is reviewed to determine whether any emergency rescues, admissions; or DOAs (dead on arrival) took place during the night. If so, a large status board in the main preparation room is reviewed for any immediate treatment or feeding instructions and orders. In addition, treatment orders and special instructions pertaining to each intensive care patient are left on this board, along with generic problems in any of the outdoor recovery yards.

Leaves are then changed, floors cleaned, patient charts in the intensive care units are reviewed for any changes in the koala patients' conditions. The ICU charts are completed several times a day, depending upon medication schedules, but at a minimum are completed at each feeding time. These charts also note all medications given, the koala's overall condition, mood, sleeping habits, appetite, intake/output, as well as any subjective observations made by the caregivers.

While this information is being recorded, other members of the crew are both readying the leaf room for distribution and cleaning up the outside yards and gunyahs (changing the water in leaf canisters), all in preparation for the koalas' evening meal. Each intensive care koala receives a mix of leaves based upon detailed knowledge of its diet prior

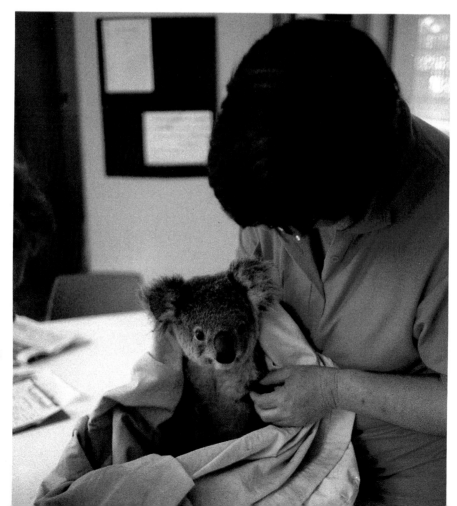

A beautiful young patient who simply had no tree to call home. The few remaining trees belonged to other dominant males. Eventually a new area was found for him by Koala Preservation Society members.

to admission, either from computer records if the koala has been in the hospital before or rescue team observations. Rescue team members must do a great deal more than the typically complicated task of bringing the koala to safety; they must make note of a number of very important data, including diet or the species of the tree the koala is found in. If this sort of information is lacking for any number of reasons, the koalas are given a variety of eucalyptus leaves, their preferences noted, and their diet modified over time. After leaf distribution, pulverized leaves, dietary supplements, and medications are prepared for all patients. A common injury to trauma victims is damage to the jaw or teeth, making eating and chewing difficult, painful, or even impossible. The most frequent cause of this is being hit by an automobile. Automobile accidents, not surprisingly, usually inflict serious injury, sometimes leading to death. Fractured bones, internal injuries, and the like are common. A hairline fracture to the jaw is a particularly disturbing injury, especially when, as is sometimes the case, it is the only injury. In this type of injury, the koala is subjected to the stress of captivity and adjustment to human contact for the relatively long period required for these fractures to heal. The case of Pebbles is illustrative.

Dietary supplements are provided for many patients who may be generally debilitated due to drought, loss of territory, or other factors.

Pebbles sustained an injury to the jaw. She can now chew, but requires supplements to her diet for adequate nutrition.

Over a year ago an emergency call came in to the hospital rescue line indicating that a koala had been hit on a local road. Several children and other spectators were standing along the roadside when the hospital rescue team arrived. The team concluded that the koala, a large female, was dead. After explaining to the group of neighbors what had happened and how frequently koalas are senselessly lost because of drivers' not heeding the specially placed signs around town indicating koala crossings, the team wrapped up the dead koala, preparing to take it to the hospital. Suddenly, a few children several feet away moved forward with a tiny bundle wrapped for warmth. They explained that they had heard the joey's plaintive cries and had found it covered in dirt and pebbles, lying in the gutter. The Koala Hospital team came over and to their astonishment immediately saw that the ball of fur, barely moving, was a joey, obviously thrown out of the mother's pouch when the accident took place. The joey's condition was critical.

Immediate action was called for, so the joey was wrapped up in one of the socklike blankets that hospital volunteers knit for the care of joeys in their spare time. The joey was rushed to the Koala Hospital, but the prognosis was not good. Covered in dust and pebbles, the joey, by then known to be a female, was barely breathing. When she did inhale, the process was labored and produced a squeaking sound: a sign of possible internal injuries. Following emergency treatment at the hospital, around-the-clock home care would definitely be required. Two of the Koala Preservation Society's most experienced caregivers offered to undertake what would be a long and probably unsuccessful effort to save the joey. After she was delicately cleaned, signs of injuries were apparent: the nose, terribly important for koalas, seemed at least partially blocked on one side. Breathing was shallow. She was largely unresponsive, though it was not known exactly how long she had been without her mother's milk, which young joeys in the pouch normally have full-time access to and require frequently. The possibility of internal injuries posed a bit of a dilemma over whether to offer food or even liquids.

In very young joeys, the generic question of the actual content of mother's milk is hopefully soon to be adequately resolved. What is known is that it is fundamentally different from the adult koala's diet of leaves. It has been suggested that the milk goes through a three-stage process during the six months the joey matures in the pouch. During this time, the oligosaccharides, or basic sugarlike components of the milk, may go through changes in level critical to the normal growth of the joey. This is an important subject and requires additional research for which there is no money available at present. What little is known is based upon the study of other marsupials; it would be reckless to assume that the process is the some in other animals, particularly one as unusual in its digestive and metabolic processes as the koala.

Pebbles, who was tossed from the pouch and abandoned when her mother was hit along the roadside by a motorist.

Before leaving the hospital, a treatment record card had to be prepared, which required a name: Pebbles. Caring for a seriously ill joey at home is not all fun. It calls for many sleepless nights preparing formula, monitoring its condition, and sometimes providing medication.

After many many weeks of care by the volunteer couple, there was good news and bad news. The good news was that Pebbles was alive and had started to put on a small amount of weight. The bad news was that something was wrong with her jaw. X-rays later revealed that probably due to the initial injury, her jaw and possibly other components of the mouth were damaged and could possibly prevent her from ever cutting her own leaves and chewing them properly—necessary for survival on her own. Consultations with the hospital's veterinarians, an orthopedic specialist, and even a dental surgeon, coupled with knowledge of past attempts at surgical correction, led to a decision not to operate. Many questions remain concerning Pebbles's future. For months, volunteers visited the hospital in the middle of the night to provide Pebbles with her formula and attempt to wean her onto leaves, beginning with the freshest and smallest leaves from the tips of branches. Pebbles eats slower than the average koala her age because of the poor alignment of her jaws. She is also significantly smaller than a koala her age. Hopefully, as the process moves along, Pebbles will someday be released, or at least set free into an area where the members of the society can keep a loving eye on her. Such things as abnormal wearing down of the teeth are a worry. Today, well over a year from that fateful day on the side of the road, Pebbles is in a large recovery yard at the hospital, where she spends her days happily high up in her favorite eucalyptus tree.

By 8:30 or 9:00 A.M., koala patients have had new leaves, fresh water, and whatever medication needed for the "night," regardless of whether they are in one of the private intensive care units or in one of the outdoor recovery yards. All intensive care patients have private rooms, with runners to climb on, several canisters of leaves, fresh water, and whatever else they might need.

Koalas sleep as many as 16 to 18 hours a day. In the hospital setting, care is taken to ensure quiet during the day so that patients may sleep. Koalas do wake up during the day, however, and periodically they will emerge from sleep, open their eyes a bit, and possibly shift their position after having fallen asleep in what is often an odd posture with limbs drooping. A light snack of a few leaves often accompanies these short periods of wakefulness.

If a patient had conjunctivitis, which requires the application of eye ointment, or needed some other treatment, as with burns and wounds, it would be brought to the treatment room adjacent to the intensive care units where these procedures are provided. The amount of trust koalas are willing to place in their human carers is truly extraordinary. Though treatments are not always painful, they can be uncomfortable. Remember that patients at the Koala Hospital are wild animals, most have never before been in captivity or in close proximity to humans, and they have powerful claws and biting power strong enough to clip small branches off of trees. Typically after a few days, the patients may shy away from having an inflamed eye bathed in saline, or ointment placed under an eyelid, but they rarely lash out or attempt to bite the hands caring for them.

Although more than a couple of meetings may be needed before the average human observes the differences, all koalas have personalities. No two are alike in their reactions to people, their environment, other koalas, food, and so on. It is very easy to become emotionally attached to such wonderful beings. In the long run, such close affection is not in the best interest of our koala patients, any more than it would be to a human patient in a human hospital. On the other hand, I believe that their knowing that they are loved is important to the healing process. Nonetheless, in order to maintain the healing process at optimum level, and spare both the koala patients and their caregivers eventual pain, working rosters at the hospital are rotated to avoid over-bonding. While a few special exceptions are made, for example, in the

Koalas can sleep in almost
any position as long as
there's a crook in a tree.

Love and healing go hand in hand, but a successful release back to the ancient eucalyptus is always the hospital's goal.

A volunteer painstakingly feeds a koala with a broken jaw.

case of a totally blind patient whose behavioral cues are based on sound and spatial relations, caregivers are not assigned to a particular patient for the length of their stay. Rosters are on continual rotation; working at the hospital one day might mean scrubbing down an intensive care unit with disinfectants, while the next day it might be holding a tiny joey, carefully releasing droplets of formula from a syringe onto its small tongue. That same night, the worker might be out at midnight on some lonely highway in the driving rain with a few coworkers attempting to rescue a mother and joey who have been chased up a power pole or, as in the case of Pebbles, possibly injured by a speeding car.

Two blind patients in otherwise excellent health acknowledge each other's presence, even when asleep.

A few of the patients die, and the others eventually must be released back to the area in which they were found. In either case, the feeling of separation and loss can be overwhelming. In an institution such as the Koala Hospital, nothing can be permitted to compromise the unique mission of the place, though I have had many moments for pause, pride, and wonderment over the remarkable successes and occasional tragedies that make up a typical day at the Koala Hospital.

During the day, the koalas are usually asleep. The hospital supervisor or team members will occasionally look in on the intensive care units, but the facility is for the most part quiet and empty, since this is actually the middle of the night for the patients. The fact that koalas are almost completely nocturnal is directly related to how little we know of their behavior. Where koalas are in captivity, even in the best of zoos, nearly nothing is known of their active behavior because the humans are home in bed when the koalas are active.

One area of the hospital is not quiet during the day: the administrative offices. In addition to routine duties, some of the society's most important activities are performed during the day. Chief among these is the educational program. Rarely a day passes without telephone calls from schools all over Australia planning trips to Port Macquarie and wishing to attend talks and lectures on koalas or requesting the society's publications. During my years visiting Port Macquarie, I've seen as many as a few hundred students sitting on the lawns of Roto House listening to lectures presented by members and officers of the society's Study Centre.

A section of the hospital has detailed displays explaining the structure and function of the koala, as well as excellent anatomical specimens. The society maintains a roster of superbly qualified members who devote hundreds of hours each year to presenting talks to school children, many of whom have traveled from as far away as Sydney or Brisbane. Often visitors from overseas are also found studying the displays at the Study Centre.

Occasionally a blind patient is awake during daylight hours, but will return to sleep until "morning," at dusk.

The public is not permitted inside the hospital nor allowed to touch the koalas. Facilities are provided that enable visitors to see the magnificent grounds of Roto House and to walk around the recovery yards. Because koalas are nocturnal, visitors must never photograph koalas using photo flash equipment. Their eyes can be seriously damaged by such light, which is several times the brightness of the automobile headlights that wreak such havoc with their lives in the wild.

During daylight hours, a variety of research projects go on around the hospital. Surveying and planning routes of koala food tree "corridors" is a monumental effort. Operation of a grid-based emergency rescue team dispatch system requires continual updating. Local residents are assisted in identifying koala food trees so as to prevent their being chopped down. Efforts are made to meet with developers, who propose the clearing of hundreds of acres of land each year. The pressures brought by the financial appeal of commercial development, by employment, and by housing demands all seem to be at odds with the need to save the koalas and their habitat.

The town of Port Macquarie is magnificently situated along the coast of the Tasman Sea, though nowhere near Tasmania. It is approximately six hours, by car, north of Sydney. With the growth of the local region, Port Macquarie has become an ideal retirement spot, with its exquisite beaches, superb climate, and friendly local atmosphere. As a result, hundreds of new homes have been built, many with swimming pools in the backyard. Early koala experiences with swimming pools proved tragic. We soon learned that koalas are so territorial that if a corridor is destroyed and a housing development put in its place, koalas—whose ancestors for hundreds of years may have passed along that land in search of trees—will continue to use the corridor, even falling into swimming pools. In theory, falling into water shouldn't prove fatal to koalas, since they can swim, but they usually can't get out of a pool and so drown. The Koala Preservation Society, in co-operation with the town council, has undertaken a major effort to alert pool owners to the need of installing at least one rope in their pools, affixed to the concrete on top of the pool's ledge. With such a rope in place, koalas can easily use their strong arms to climb out of the water. This avoids tragedy and trauma for all involved.

Another problem related to the encroachment on koala territory by humans is pets. Hardly a week goes by that a koala isn't brought to the hospital badly bitten or even killed by a dog. Once again, in theory at least, such encounters shouldn't prove fatal—koalas are well equipped to ward off a dog or even a fiercer animal. But because of the lack of natural predators in Australia, koalas have not had experience with the need for self-defense, and they rarely defend themselves against attacking dogs. In addition, because of their undersized adrenals, they are unlikely to muster the "fight/flight" reaction typical of other mammals when attacked. A koala can suffer terrible stress from such an encounter. I've helped rescue koalas that have been chased by dogs up flagpoles, high-tension utility lines, commercial construction sites, and various other unnatural heights. Even if they haven't been bitten, such koalas are usually in shock when brought to the hospital and require many days of rest. Some of these patients die from no apparent cause, and we can only assume such deaths are a result of stress.

By 3:30 P.M. the busiest and largest team of the day arrives at the hospital. As in the morning, all units receive fresh leaves from the leaf rooms and fresh water. All patient charts are updated and reviewed for any treatment orders that may have been added or modified by veterinarians or other specialists who have come by since the early morning

Koalas will fall into swimming pools constructed in the paths of their former food tree corridors, some of which may have existed for hundreds of years. A rope attached to the side can provide a grip and will save a koala's life.

Smaller koalas recovering outdoors but unable to chew are brought into the hospital for feeding and checkups.

shift. The treatment blackboard is similarly reviewed for changes and additions. Patients requiring weighing are placed on top of one of two unusual scales. The scale used for weighing joeys is actually a pediatric scale for humans. Fully grown patents are weighed by placing them in a large canvas bag, then placing the bag on a scale with a hook attached.

Detailed records of weight, condition of coat, and signs of dehydration are just a few of many variables critical to monitoring the conditions of patients who have come in suffering from malnutrition, intestinal disorders, or other conditions often not as yet diagnosed. Sudden weight loss or the inability to gain weight does not bode well for a creature the size of, or having a diet as specialized as, the koala.

By the time the sun is setting, all but the most ill patients are awake and very alert. Those who have been in the hospital for any period of time know that it is time for their "breakfast," as this is the start of their nocturnal day. More medication and treatment procedures are usually carried out at this time. Any unusual changes in patient conditions are noted on individual charts as well as on the hospital log, which also serves as an overnight watch book.

Most emergency admissions take place during the evening, since this is when koalas are active. When a koala is brought to the hospital by one of the society's rescue teams, details of its condition are noted in red ink in the log. In addition, a new patient record form is initiated, and unless the koala is too injured or upset, a plastic ear tag bearing a serial number is permanently attached. Females are tagged in the right ear, males in the left, so that after animals are released, at least their sex and whether or not they have been patients can be known from a distance using binoculars. From this point on, the koala's progress is tracked by the hospital's medical records system, and eventually by the computerized database. Rescue teams are trained to look for the ear tags, which are usually of a bright color, since if a patient is a re-admission, a complete treatment history, as well as dietary data, can be quickly retrieved. This can save hours of long work, examinations, and guesswork. Similarly, initial diagnostic work will be guided by the possibility of a recurring condition. Eventually, should resources become available, these records could be of invaluable use in compiling statistical models of treatment effectiveness, habitat variables, correlation between admissions and habitat destruction/preservation, climatic events, and much more.

With all treatments completed, feeding taken care of, yards cleaned, and patients accounted for (occasionally patients like to "trick" the humans by doing things such hiding on the small roofs above shelters in the yards), the treatment areas of the hospital are again

"Find the koala." The koala's superb camouflage can make rescues difficult.

scrubbed or mopped with antiseptic solutions. Inventory levels of all medications, dietary supplements, and emergency items frequently used are verified, and orders to be placed the following day are drawn up.

Before the afternoon shift leaves for the night, a special telecommunications system is activated: essentially an emergency action notification system. A local telephone number is published and made known throughout the region for use in reporting any sort of emergency involving koalas. The police, electrical utility, and other civil service providers also have the number at hand. Should a call come in after the afternoon shift has gone for the night, these calls are automatically routed to the night rescue roster. All such teams have a full complement of rescue tools, making an initial run to the hospital to pick up such gear unnecessary. In addition, the night roster team leaders have keys to the hospital facilities, allowing for a smooth emergency admission process.

Great care must be exercised in rescuing koalas. Not only may the animal be seriously injured, but it may act aggressively toward its rescuer. If fully conscious, it may scratch and bite, and it has the potential of

A curious and cunning koala takes to the roof of a gunyah.

inflicting serious injury to a human, about whom the koala knows nothing, probably never having seen one before. In addition, with most emergency rescues occurring in the evening or night hours, rescuers must often work alongside unlighted highways or walk into areas with thick underbrush.

Over the years, remarkably effective methods have been devised for rescuing koalas. While effective, these procedures require practice, strength, patience, and good reflexes. As a rule, they cannot be performed by a single volunteer. Good teamwork is essential to the effort. Different techniques are employed depending on where the injury has taken place and whether the koala is high above the ground or lying injured on the roadside, as was the case with Pebbles. Untrained persons should definitely not attempt to rescue or pick up an ill or injured koala. It may be of some comfort to North Americans to know that, as in England, rabies does not exist in Australia.

Cases such as Pebbles raise profoundly difficult ethical questions in the management of threatened and endangered species. First, without the highly unusual care provided by the Koala Preservation Society, Pebbles would not have survived. With the likelihood of her long-term chances for release and full independence guarded at best, because of her jaw problem, not to mention a possibly long and painful recovery, would it not be kinder, in the long run, for her to be euthanized? What about limited space and funds available to the hospital? Shouldn't they be made available to koalas with a better prognosis and shorter recovery period? These are nasty questions, indeed, but important policy issues when dealing with one of the world's oldest remaining inhabitants and one not at all free from threat of extinction. In the final analysis, the society makes extraordinary efforts to give every patient more than a fighting chance. Animals are put down only on veterinary decisions when a diagnosis of cancer, terminal injury, or some similar fate has been confirmed, or when the koala is in pain from an unmanageable or untreatable condition. As with the better human hospitals, Koala Hospital patients are not turned away for lack of space, resources, or even health insurance!

Dead animals are frozen and sent by special courier to the Department of Veterinary Pathology at the University of Sydney, where they are autopsied or otherwise used for instructional purposes. When particularly complex or undiagnosable disease is suspected, sophisticated pathology, hematology, and immunology studies are carried out, with results sent to the hospital.

During one of my first "tours of duty" at the Koala Hospital, an emergency admission was brought in. A fully developed male koala was semicomatose, with near normal vital signs, but with slightly depressed respiration. Despite an eyewitness account that he had been hit at least once by an automobile, a detailed examination revealed no laceration or broken bones. More by deduction than induction, I suggested that the koala patient was possibly suffering from a subdural hematoma, pressure from which was suppressing signals leaving the motor area of the brain going to muscular systems. Although hospital workers with far more experience than I reported a very poor prognosis based on past experience, I was indulged and allowed to care for the koala, now named New Yorker after my distant and so different hometown. Several weeks passed during which New Yorker's lassitude remained pervasive. His total lack of motivation, desire to eat or remain awake, even during the normal six hours of waking time, made caring for him difficult and, over time, discouraging. Finally, before I left the hospital that year, New Yorker started to show signs of improvement. He would move his hands and legs, though the energetic walking around normal to koalas was nowhere to be seen.

The probability of a total recovery, so necessary for a koala who must forage high in eucalyptus trees, often delicately balanced on moving branches, was unknown. After many months of loving (and expensive) care by the volunteers at the Koala Hospital, New Yorker was released. Perhaps this long recovery time, which is not short even in mammals, such as humans, that have extensive corpus callosums, is due to the absence in koalas of this important cable linking the two halves of the brain.

FIRE! THE STORY OF TERRY GLEN

THE MIDDLE OF the day is usually a quiet time at the Koala Hospital. The morning team has long finished providing fresh leaves for the koalas. Medications and formulas have been given, and all utensils have been washed and put away, including the formula bowls, each of which bears a patient's name. On one particular day, a beautiful day in spring, one could hear Fenig and Long Flat, two magnificent but totally blind males, as they moved around in the yard they shared and made occasional grunts. The building was full of the distinctive clean odor that is a combination of the disinfectants used to wash the floors and the strong eucalyptus scent given off by the koalas and the leaves. In all, the hospital seemed a pleasant and relaxing place to spend the early afternoon. I was sitting in the main preparation room sipping a cup of tea with

Judy, the hospital supervisor, who was about to leave to attend to some errands. Then the phone rang. Telephone calls are usually answered in the administrative offices during the day. The emergency notification system, which diverts calls to night rescue teams, was not activated. Rescue calls are infrequent during the day, of course, since the koalas are happily asleep high in their trees.

But the phones kept ringing; for some reason no one was answering. Thinking that the office staff might have gone over to the National Parks office to use the photocopy machine, Judy picked up the phone. She listened in silence and then asked a series of short, abrupt questions: "Where?" "How large an area is involved?" "How many homes?" "How long has it been going?" and finally, "I'll have to get a crew out right away, but we'll have to notify Oxley Electric." I couldn't imagine what she was talking about and thought only that perhaps a koala had gone up an electric pole, which they sometimes do when chased by dogs.

She hung up and quickly explained to me that a large forest fire had broken out across town near the old race track, that several newly constructed homes were within a short distance of the fire, and that fire teams were responding from several nearby towns. She said the houses would be at risk if the winds—often strong at that time of the year—shifted, and that evacuation might have to be ordered.

Visibly shaken, she added, "What is more, we've been releasing koalas over there for quite some time. It's one of the few areas left where there are—or were—many of the right trees for them." I asked her how many koalas had been released, and she said a couple dozen.

Telephone calls continued to come in from people who lived in that part of town, sounding the alarm. Many homeowners had seen release teams in the past carrying their canvas bags containing rehabilitated koalas going off into the woods, and they now realized that a major tragedy might be in the offing.

Over the past several years, the local electric company had generously allowed its cherry pickers to be used in rescuing koalas. Those huge machines—with their long extendible arms with buckets—are unbeatable for rescuing koalas from trees, power lines, construction sites, and other high and hard-to-reach places.

Daytime emergencies present special problems. Nearly everyone is either busy with family responsibilities or at work on their regular jobs—

The author with Terry Glen after over a year of treatment for critical injuries sustained in a bush fire.

including, of course, the electric company. Judy made frantic calls to team leaders, members in that area, and her husband in an effort to round up at least a basic complement of society members to form a fire rescue team. She also called the Oxley Electric Company in the hope of getting some help. The company dispatcher already knew about the fire, since the police and fire departments had asked that the power be shut down to reduce the potential hazard from wires that had come loose or been knocked down by the fire. He also reported that all the company's crews were busy. Judy explained that it had been many weeks since the last rain and that many koalas were known to be in the area of the fire, and the dispatcher promised he'd contact the depot supervisor and call us back. Not five minutes later a call came through from the supervisor, who reported that two men with an extra-length cherry picker had been contacted by radio and redeployed to the scene. He added, however, that the fire brigades were reporting heavy smoke and that electric company crews are under explicit instructions not to enter fire zones or place company equipment—or themselves—at risk.

As we drove from the hospital through town we could see that the sky on the other side of town was a brownish orange. The closer we got, the more intense the smoke became. Following the supervisor's directions, we approached the area through the newly constructed housing development. "This looks really bad," said Judy, getting out of the car and taking a quick look around. "They'll be dead if they didn't get out." Other society members had already arrived and were staring blankly at the burnt-out forest, which began about 70 feet behind the new houses.

I thought we had arrived too late, that we'd heard of the fire after it was mostly over, but I was quickly told that fires involving eucalyptus trees are essentially flash fires but that because of the combustibility of the trees' sap, they are also practically explosive. I was also surprised to learn that these brief but intense fires do not permanently destroy the forests; they destroy only the underbrush. In the overall scheme of things, these fires have been part of nature's important cycles in Australia for tens of thousands of years.

With instructions to fan out in a matrix and be on the lookout for any signs of koala life, our teams of society members began walking toward the perimeter of the burnt-out forest. I walked into the forest beside Judy, who told me some terrible realities. Fires are devastating to

Woods where koalas were known to live before a bush fire (above), and after the fire.

koalas, and not only because they wipe out their food trees. Fires force koalas farther and farther up trees, and even if not burned, they suffer the awful effects of smoke inhalation. Smoke can permanently damage the olfactory nerves, which are responsible for their senses of smell and taste and critical to their ability to determine which are the correct leaves to eat. Smoke can also damage the epithelial tissue of the nose and windpipe. This is smooth skin similar to what humans feel inside their mouths if they run their tongues along the insides of their cheeks. These tissues are very sensitive and can swell up, choking off breathing within the windpipe. I could see no signs of life in the trees, but I could feel heat from the tree trunks on my face as I walked by one charred eucalyptus after another. How amazing that these forests regenerate—and how tragic, I thought, that the koalas probably never will.

One of the women with us stopped and pointed up at a black mass on top of a tree. "Do you think that's a koala?" she asked. A nearby volunteer fireman said it was probably only a mass of sap. He explained that the intense heat of fires pulls out the sap, which partially burns and then forms round, bubblelike shapes. The two men from the electric company, Glen and Terry, were walking along with us, and one of them added that the ground was still smoldering and it was not yet safe enough to consider bringing the cherry picker in. The heat could make the tires melt or burst.

Although the production of smoke had stopped, the smell was overwhelming. The scene before us was startling. A recent volcanic eruption that had taken place thousands of miles away in the Philippines had filled the high-altitude atmosphere with dust, and it had been producing magnificent sunsets. But now, as the sun began its daily descent, the color of the sky and the desolation around me made me realize that I was seeing something for the first time, something others had seen in this amazing land for tens of thousands of years. This, I thought, was what parts of the earth would look like after humans blew the place up, and it was also what parts of Australia must have looked like, at least temporarily, after lightning had ignited the fires referred to in Aboriginal mythology.

"I think it moved!" one of our party called out. I looked up and saw no movement, but I remembered my poor track record trying to locate koalas in trees on various society outings. I sensed that our group felt so useless, standing there in the dead forest, that some kind of action had to be taken to justify the effort. Glen and Terry said they'd attempt to bring their cherry picker in. I didn't think they'd succeed and thought it would be a lot of effort for nothing, but I decided to remain quiet, sensing that everyone would feel better later, having at least done something. It was clear to everyone that wending that piece of heavy equipment between the dozens of closely spaced burned trees was going to be a major challenge. But Glen said it would be good practice.

We all doubted that the black object high in the tree was any life form, or even a previous life form, but the "exercise" went forward. We watched in amazement as Terry, driving the cherry picker, maneuvered it between the trees.

It took about 20 minutes for the cherry picker to reach the base of the tree. Long arms extended from the sides of the machine and rested on circular pods on the ground to provide support and keep the machine from toppling over as its long arm with two buckets carried Terry and Glen higher and higher into the trees. The procedure had to be interrupted several times so that the base of the machine could rotate the extended arm out of the way of the remaining branches high above us.

By now Terry and Glen were so high up in the trees that I had to use the telephoto lens of my camera to make out their activities. When they reached the black mass they signaled two thumbs up; I saw the motion through my lens and relayed the news to the rest of the group. I interpreted this to mean they had found a koala. Judy, who always fears the worst in situations but has an unspoken and unrelenting faith in positive outcomes, said, "Aw, but it'll be dead, or if it isn't, we'll have to put it down. A koala could never survive a thing like this."

One of the men (I couldn't tell which) held a canvas rescue bag, while the other gently lifted the black mass into the bag. The trip up had taken about ten minutes, but Terry, Glen, and the sack made the return descent in about thirty seconds.

Indeed a koala was in the bag. All his fur was charred, and he smelled terrible. The fur around his ears was gone. His nose was peeling. His eyelashes were gone, revealing pink skin, but surprisingly he was breathing, though shallowly. Leaving the rest of our crew and Terry and

Glen to continue the search, though it would soon be dark, Judy and I rushed to the surgical suite of the hospital's chief veterinarian. He was not to be found, but his wife, Dr. Karen Fripp, also an outstanding and sensitive veterinarian, was elsewhere in the building and was called to the scene.

I was fairly certain that our patient was in deep physical shock but had no idea how the process of hydration, electrolyte balancing, and prevention of infection, which I knew were prime emergency treatment objectives in humans, could be carried out in koalas. Intravenous drips do not do well in koalas. Their veins are not easy to locate and often will not support an IV. Obviously, a wild animal will not leave an IV line in place for very long either.

Karen Fripp commented that koalas had very baggy skin on their backs and that perhaps she could place an IV there and fill the space up with saline solution on the chance that this would at least stabilize things for a while. She said the process could take hours. After this was done, antibiotics that could be used would have to be found. Remember that koalas have a unique digestive system, that their leaves are quite toxic and difficult to digest, and that if the intestinal fora were to be destroyed by antibiotics, the animal could die from the problems this would create. Paraffin bandages would have to be applied to the burned areas and changed every few hours for weeks if our koala were to survive. In addition, where the hands, tail, and nose were burned, a special preparation made in Switzerland and used in treating humans would have to be obtained as soon as possible.

Our patient was getting weaker and "waxy." This means that if an arm or leg were moved, it would sort of stay there or drop back to its normal position very slowly, as if it were made of wax: not at all normal for a koala. The veterinarians agreed that we should try the intravenous saline solution running into the space under the fur on the back. Along with Dr. Fripp, we took turns for hours, standing on the treatment table acting as human IV supports, while the saline quickly dripped. After nearly two hours, our patient was at least still alive and seemed a bit more alert. While I held the bag of saline, the hospital supervisor and Dr. Fripp applied ointment and bandages, which would have to be changed in a few hours. Little booties were cut of cotton cloth, with medication-soaked pads inside for the burned feet, which had lost all of their important claws in the fire.

I knew that one of the greatest risks with human burn patients was that of infection. I didn't know how big a problem this was with koalas. Dr. Fripp said that after we took our patient to the hospital, he would require not only a very quiet space, change of dressing every four or so hours, as much liquid as possible, and warmth, but he could not be taken out of doors probably for months, since air-borne spores and bacteria could launch a catastrophic infection. We didn't even know if, as is sometimes the case, the delayed swelling of the windpipe would set in. I asked whether corticosteroid anti-inflammatory medications were used in this situation and was told that it was a good idea but possibly too risky. Dosages and sensitivities were not known. Ultimately, a small dose of an anti-inflammatory drug was given. We felt that we had little chance of success but were deeply moved by our patient's sitting for hours, letting humans work on him.

After a few bags of saline solution had trickled into our patient and he was bandaged, it was time to take him to what was to become his home for the next year: the Koala Hospital. He couldn't walk on his own because the bandages on his feet eliminated any traction his feet might have had. We bundled him up in blankets and placed him in a large basket similar to a laundry basket; these are often used to transport critical patients, as other supporting objects can be used to prop up the koalas so that they can breathe properly. Temperature is maintained with hot water bottles. Before leaving, Dr. Fripp remembered that no paper-work had been completed, due to the urgency with which our patient needed treatment. The first item on the treatment forms reminded us that we had never given our special patient a name. There was no debate, for it was obvious that the koala would have died in the tree had it not been for the amazing skill of the two men from the Oxley Electric Company. From then on our patient was known as Terry Glen.

The local surgical and hospital supply company had only a limited number of paraffin bandages and only two tubes of the recently developed white ointment that needed to be applied several times a day to Terry Glen's nose and feet. Clearly this would not suffice. I explained to the company's owner that we had a critically burned koala. He promised to have a case of the paraffin bandages expressed from Sydney the following day, but the ointment was a "no go." Since the medicine was nowhere to be found and was made in Switzerland, I decided to call the pharmaceutical company in Basel. I thought I would ask for a humanitarian donation of the medicine for our special patient.

At the hospital, Terry Glen was given his own room in the intensive care unit after it had been supplied with an abundant supply of leaves, fresh water, and a large basket for him to use as a "bed" should he be too weak to sit in the branches. It was not clear whether he would be able to remain on the runners, as most of his claws had been lost in the fire; his feet were now totally bandaged. Loss of claws in fires is a serious problem, for although they usually grow back over a long period of time, they often do not grow back properly. Sometimes they return at odd angles, making them relatively useless for the koalas, who must rely on them for climbing. We were afraid he might fall off his perch and hurt himself on the hard floor, which was covered only with newspaper and taped padding on the main runner in his unit.

At first we decided to place him in the crook of the large log forming the main crossbar of his indoor home, since this, with the leaves all around, would be most like his normal habitat. When I held out some leaves to him, he ate them quite voraciously. Most people might see this behavior as a good sign, but over time, we have seen stressed koalas do exactly this: gorge themselves. This is some sort of syndrome, as they may then stop eating altogether and eventually die. This pattern is not well understood and should be researched further. Thus, Terry Glenn's early eating did not give us much comfort.

Plans had to be made for his care. While the hospital supervisor was most skilled at changing the bandages, debriding the burned tissue, applying fresh paraffin bandages, and making our special patient feel very cared for, unless we did something quickly all would be lost for lack of medication.

When I telephoned the pharmaceutical company in Basel, Switzerland, and explained our dire circumstances, I received an incredulous response: "A *what* hospital?" I explained what koalas were, that I had lived in the Zurich area for a few years, and that no, there were no koalas in the Zurich Zoo up above the university. Finally, I was connected to a vice president in the part of the company responsible for manufacturing the medication. Despite my poor Swiss German, he understood my story, but to my great frustration he didn't believe it. He said he had never heard of a hospital just for koalas, that the drugs required a medical prescription from a physician, not a veterinarian, and that unless he had some hard evidence supporting this entire *unglaublish* ("totally unbelievable") affair, there was nothing he could do. He hung up.

An idea immediately occurred to me: take a photograph of Terry Glen, all sad and burned, and send it to him. It was surely a desperate sight and might melt the ice in this man's heart. I did just that and took the role of film to a local photoshop that advertised they could process film in three hours. I faxed, and mailed, the photo to Switzerland and phoned back the next morning. "Ah, yes, the koala doctor, we have already called our distributor in Australia and alerted them to a carton of the drug being shipped by air. It will still take most of a week, and you will have to pay costs through the Australian distributor. Will one carton be enough?" I asked for two to be safe and said that we could try to find some locally through human hospitals until his shipment arrived. The two human hospitals in town were at least aware of our existence and had known several society members who had worked as hospital volunteers.

It was decided that I would come in after I had my evening meal and check on Terry Glen, change bandages if needed, and then come back at 1:00 or 2:00 A.M. and repeat the process. The morning roster of workers and probably the hospital supervisor would handle things in the morning. Fortunately, what New Yorkers and koalas have in common is a nocturnal life style. So I had no objection to spending quiet evenings sitting alone in the hospital with my furry friends and knowing that Terry Glen was okay . . . hopefully.

For the first few weeks Terry Glen sat gently and very sadly. I would look in on him every two or three hours. One evening I went in to see how things were going and thought that his nose needed some more white salve. When I applied it, his nose felt terribly hot. I panicked and was sure that my worst fear, infection, had become a reality. I called the hospital supervisor at home, knowing that this wouldn't exactly win me many "brownie points," but too worried to let that bother me.

"Terry Glen's nose is very hot," I urgently reported. Instead of expressing any alarm, the sleepy voice said only, "So what?" I was told to go back in ten minutes and that in all probability his nose would be cool again. "Koalas do that, don't cha know?" As always, she was right. His nose was perfectly cool to the touch; I am sure Terry Glen wondered why I was going in there touching his nose, and the supervisor wondered why in the world I had called in the middle of the night with such an observation. I wanted to talk and comfort our patient, but he was asleep—or so I thought. As I was leaving his unit, I remembered that I had left the tube of medicine on the ledge and turned to pick it up. I could have sworn that Terry Glen moved his head, but if so he was too fast for me. I slowly moved out of the unit, hiding behind the door. Slowly he opened an eye. When I looked around the door, it snapped shut. He was playing with me, feigning sleep. A trickster at heart! I gave him a few scratches behind the ears, which koalas seem to like and find relaxing, told him that we all loved him, and left, shutting the light off in the intensive care unit.

The next drama with Terry Glen was a bit more real. Though my "hours" were in the early morning, I would come in to the hospital each day around 10:00 A.M. to visit with the supervisor, assist the attending veterinarians and any specialists on call with treatments, and sometimes have lunch with the volunteers working in the small shop at the hospital. When I arrived, the supervisor said to me, "You're not going to be very happy." She went on to explain that Terry Glen had stopped eating and had become less responsive. She said she had seen this before several times with koalas who had to be hospitalized for long periods of time and that they usually became very depressed and often did not recover.

As days went by, he became worse and increasingly unresponsive with his head just sort of drooping down; I was getting about as depressed over the prospect of losing Terry Glen. Judy, the supervisor whose intuition concerning the care of the koalas I trusted implicitly, just said, "They can't be away from the trees for too long. They need to see the trees." I thought this was a bit curious, as I remembered from years before when visiting the home of Jean Starr, the society's founder, that blinds had to be installed in a holding area where koalas could otherwise see the trees outside. Jean had told me that if they saw the trees, the koalas would scratch at the window and possibly hurt them-

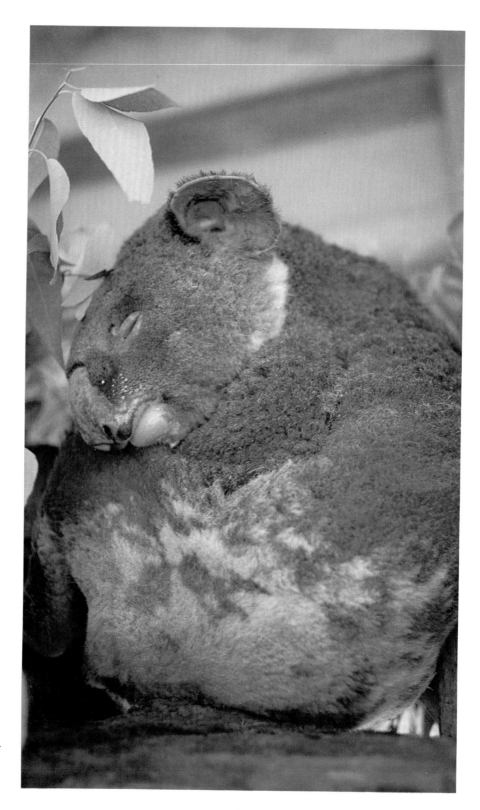

A despondent Terry Glen recovering in the Intensive Care Unit. Note loss of hair on eyes, eyelids, and other areas.

selves. I guess Terry Glen was just too weak or depressed for this sort of thing.

I felt torn between simply following orders, which called for quiet and continued care in his own intensive care unit, and my tendency as a psychologist to "project" and treat Terry Glen as a human patient, thinking that he was terribly depressed from lack of stimulation and from isolation. The more time I spent with Terry Glen, visiting with him frequently and finding him less and less responsive to my pep talks and scratching behind the ears, the more I felt that aggressive measures had to be taken. By this point he was hardly eating and was losing weight slowly: a bad omen, indeed. Admittedly I had become quite attached to the little fellow, who by the way, for a koala, was not small. I felt that some of the workers were backing away emotionally, fearing the worst and not wanting to get attached, while I was doing the reverse.

I proposed to the hospital supervisor that since there appeared to be little to lose, I wanted to take Terry Glen for a walk. That idea met with raised eyebrows and a long silence of disapproval. The risk from this action could be infection from air-borne spores and other things. I took one of the blankets made especially for the koalas out of the supply cabinet, wrapped him up, and placed him on a few towels, which I had draped over my shoulder. I almost didn't proceed, as when I picked him up, he grunted. We walked around the inside of the hospital, which didn't seem to please him in any great way. It was a beautiful clear, cool day, with a little wind rustling through the high eucalyptus trees surrounding the hospital. I then walked out the front door and around the front yard of the hospital.

Immediately, I could feel his muscle tone change. He shifted and perked up, looking upward at the trees. Judy had been right, once again. I was afraid that he might try vigorously to get away, but he just hugged me some more. I guess he was too weak. Stopping at several trees, I broke off small branches and offered them to him. Not interested. He made a couple of koala grunts, which I mimicked and he liked, or at least returned. I was relieved to see him take some interest in the outside world and react to it, though I knew trouble lay ahead in trying to convince others of the wisdom of these excursions. He was also responding to the calls of Australia's magnificent birds, which are all around the hospital.

A few years before all of this, the society, in a very thoughtful gesture, planted a tree in memory of my close friend whom I had met on the computer network. It is near the hospital, in front of Roto House. A small plaque memorializes Jim Faison, a gifted musician, photographer, and computer programmer. I thought that it might be nice to introduce Terry Glen to what had become known as the "Jimmy Tree," and vice versa. I debated staying out, however, for Terry Glen had not been eating properly for several weeks at this point. Having decided not to tell anyone about our clandestine excursion, I decided to walk over to the Jimmy Tree. The tree was still only slightly taller than I was—about six feet—too small to support a koala's weight or food requirements. I broke off a small branch with a few very fresh reddish new leaves on it, and to my amazement, he gobbled them right away. From that point on, Terry Glen continued to eat. I thought it would make my friend Jimmy very happy to know that his tree spurred a very special koala into eating again!

With Terry Glen eating again, I was sleeping a lot better, for in the back of my mind I knew that my annual visit with my "children"—as my friends referred to the koalas—would soon be coming to an end. The tremendous psychological effect on Terry Glen of taking him outdoors for his first walk was very uplifting. Several brief walks followed almost every day, and eventually, we enjoyed hour-long visits simply sitting together in the sun. These established what Judy had told me long before: Koalas need the stimulation of their natural environment and should not, in illness or health, be placed in captivity for a second longer than absolutely necessary. It is not surprising that koalas in zoos live significantly shorter and, I insist, unhappier lives. The difference all of this made in the course of Terry Glenn's progress was so dramatic that one cannot help but be impressed with how important it is to ensure that koalas remain free ranging and not captive to the whims of humans for entertainment, amusement, curiosity, or worse.

Each year I dread the day of leaving my friends in Port Macquarie, who are always so giving of their patience and hospitality. Particularly difficult was knowing that for a year I would be away from the koalas, separated by a six-hour drive to Sydney, a seventeen-hour flight to California, and another five-hour flight to New York. The separation is always painful, for throughout the year I experience nothing similar to the relationship I have with the koalas. By the time departure day came, Terry Glen had been outdoors in one of the recovery yards for a few weeks and was doing reasonably well. He still required bandages on two feet, and Judy and other volunteers had devoted hundreds of hours of care to debriding his burns and bathing his feet in iodine solutions, while I took care of the late-night duties. Terry Glen knew his caregivers well. Even before he and I began our regular excursions outside, when I would enter his unit in the evening, he would put his hands up in the air, signaling he wanted to be picked up and carried for a ride. This type of relationship with a human, contrary to what most people think, is very unusual. Koalas are usually aloof.

My car was packed, and I'd had a nice farewell dinner the night before with close friends from the hospital. I drove to the hospital to say my good-byes and, of course, to visit with the patients. Terry Glen was up in his gunyah, sitting on the end of it actually, chewing. I know my more experienced friends at the hospital consider some of my behavior odd— for example, talking with the koalas and making their calls—but I stood at the end of the gunyah, gave Terry Glen a few scratches behind the ear, and explained that I had to go home, but that lots of loving people would continue to take good care of him and that I thought he was wonderful and thanked him for letting me take care of him. I was surprised when he placed his right front foot on the left cheek of my face and gave me little pats. This show of affection went on for a few minutes, after which he gave a rather strong shove, which I took as a message to get going, not knowing if I would ever again see him. This is always a dilemma with our patients, for in truth we should hope to never see them again, since doing so would mean that they are in trouble. We rubbed noses, and then I left Port Macquarie for another year.

During that year, as I had promised, Terry Glen received magnificent care from a dedicated team of workers at the hospital. I telephoned every couple of weeks and always inquired about Terry Glen, who was making excellent, though slow, progress. Burns take a long time to heal and fur requires a long time to grow back. Probably most difficult was the process of ensuring that enough nails would grow back and straight enough for him to eventually be released into the wild, where he would be happiest. The members of the society wrote to me, enclosing photographs documenting Terry Glen's progress. Ironically, during this time I

Terry Glen is eager to see
visitors after nine months of
"TLC" and successful
treatment.

developed a foot infection requiring well over two weeks of hospitalization and the surgical removal of part of one toe, followed by days of intravenous antibiotic therapy. The pictures of Terry Glen, some of which are shared here, represent a very special bond and helped me weather that experience. His story (and his picture sitting bedside) also fascinated nurses, technicians, and my surgeon and his wife, leading to a very valued friendship.

As the year went by, it was clear that Terry Glen represented a rather remarkable success, owing to the major team effort. Also, it was clear that he would soon be ready to be released. Putting burn patients back in the wild, one of the most important precepts of the society's work, presents a difficult problem, since their original territory is generally rendered unsuitable for habitation. Being highly territorial, koalas cannot simply be left in unfamiliar territory where, in all probability, another dominant male has already staked out turf. Members of the society had spent a great deal of time finding an area not terribly far from where the fire had been that seemed suitable. It had a variety of koala food trees in it, did not appear to be territory belonging to any other koalas, seemed to have low susceptibility to fire, and was large and relatively secluded from humans. The reason why bonding with humans is usually avoided is that the koalas may seek out humans after release. Although most humans today would not harm a koala, as they once did, their pets will. An effort is therefore made to find the best possible habitat for release of koalas.

About a week after my arrival the following year—and after an exuberant greeting by Terry Glen who definitely remembered me—we felt there was no reason for him to remain any longer in the hospital. He was in fine shape. All of his fur had grown back magnificently; most of his nails were back; his mood was excited. The hospital supervisor had been telling him that his favorite human was coming back to release him soon. I thought it only appropriate to invite Terry and Glen, the two remarkable men from the electric company, to join the society members who were going out to release Terry Glen. Thus, one bright and warm morning Terry, Glen, the hospital supervisor, a couple of members who had spent many late and hard hours with Terry Glen, and I, drove to the release site.

Terry and Glen carried the large canvas bag used for transporting koalas into the wooded area for release, while I manned television and still cameras. When the rope closing the top of the sack was loosened,

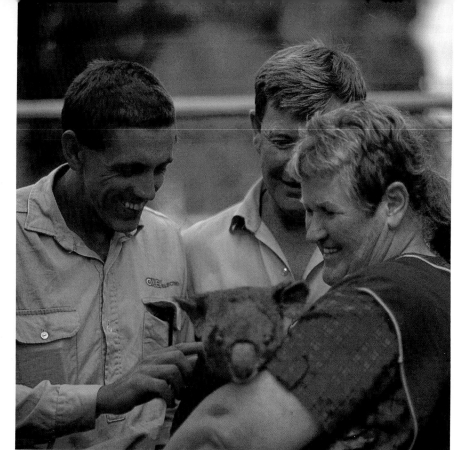

Terry and Glen, who rescued the eponymous koala from a burning tree, and the hospital supervisor are delighted with his progress, though his ears remain bare.

Terry Glen about to return to the world of the forests after a year in the hospital.

out popped an exuberant Terry Glen with a wonderful "smile" on his face. He took one look around and went directly for the tree. Still not sure of his footing with his new nails, he slowly climbed up and sat on a branch about ten feet above the ground and watched us carefully. We packed up our gear, wished Terry Glen happiness and love, and left.

A few times during that year's visit, I drove down that dirt road, looking for my furry friend. People living a couple of miles away had called the hospital to report hearing loud koala calls during breeding season; they said they had never heard such sounds before. By now, there is at least one, and possibly several, Terry Glen, Juniors. Though I have never seen Terry Glen since that joyous day of his release, he frequently visits my dreams, leaving me with a wonderful feeling of having met a kindred spirit.

A magnificent Terry Glen gives a final glance to his departing human caregivers before jumping into a eucalyptus tree, his new home.

KOALAS, THE DREAMTIME, AND THE CREATION OF THE EARTH

Throughout Australia the traditional Aboriginal people treated the koala with respect, and in some areas it was completely taboo, and so was never hunted or harmed. The people of South Eastern Australia have a legend to explain this.

—Jean A. Ellis, Eugowra
"From the Dreamtime"

According to lore, all beings, whether young or old souls, are inextricably linked to the Dreamtime forces.

In order to understand the koala as more than an increasingly scarce marsupial that happens to live in Australia, one must become familiar with the world view held by one of the oldest clusters of cultures on our planet: the Australian Aborigines. Many thousands of years old, this understanding of existence, which predates the great civilizations of China, Rome, and Greece, prefigured many concepts and experiences

just now being discovered, or "rediscovered," at the frontiers of physics, astronomy, and psychology.

This claim may seem variously ridiculous, mystical, or unscientific to those encountering early cultures or modern theories of cosmogony for the first time, but I believe that such patterns of patterns are to be expected. Experiencing the implicit orderliness of the universe requires both the ability, unique to animal life, to process information gathered by the senses and, of course, the phenomena themselves. As knowledge becomes increasingly compartmentalized or specialized in our technologically based culture, perceptions of universal order become significantly more difficult and unlikely. It is therefore not at all surprising that the members of native cultures, such as the Australian Aborigines and North American Indians, who passed along oral traditions, were on so much more intimate terms with these ideas than we are today. Understandably, it is a bit difficult to behold the unifying powers of the universe when one receives an average of 15 telephone calls a day at the office, spends at least four hours a day watching television, owes an average of $1,700 on a credit card, and has to make monthly payments on a car or two and a home that in the previous year may have lost 11 percent of its value: all fairly commonplace worries for the average American.

For the initiated Aborigine, it was very important to experience rather than just perceive the unifying factors in the world. Anthropologists, psychologists, art historians, and philosophers have written of such things for a long time. In attempting to discover what the earliest inhabitants of the place we now call Australia knew of some of the planet's earliest animals, I found a group of tribal, agrarian cultures with traditions of myth, symbols, and sound that were as subtle as they were complex. Because humans appear to be unique among the animal species principally because of their ability to process information analogically, the study of metaphor through myth and symbol is important. I don't believe that these capacities are exclusively human, as I have lived, slept, healed, and played with other animals as common as dogs and as exotic as koalas and have observed such behaviors as dreaming and even primitive problem solving in all of them.

Because most humans conceive of time in a linear manner, we tend to think that everything has a "beginning" and an "end." The Australian

The existence of koalas in
Australia began thousands of
years before the arrival of
man, which, according to
myth, could not have
happened without koala.

Aborigines' traditions are a most impressive exception to this perception. Aboriginal culture, which goes back 120,000 to 150,000 years, may represent the oldest and most profound representation of the collective human experience. The native traditions assumed as a given that the earth and all of its inhabitants were intrinsically alike. According to Aboriginal understanding, the earth was created long ago, during a time when massive forces of the Universe were focused here and wandered the globe, forming the land masses, oceans, and all first life forms. The time when all of this happened was called the Dreamtime. All that exists and lives today owes its heritage to the forces of the Dreamtime. These forces are unique, discrete, and by nature infinite as to strength. For this reason, certain spaces, the first life forms, and rituals are sacred. Tragically, in both North America and Australia, after thousands of years of practice, these traditions were in a short period of time overridden, nearly to the point of extinction, by British colonialization and the industrialization and growth that followed.

The Aboriginal groups had intimate and profound initiation rites. Those initiated into the knowledge were typically given two names. One was a "personal name," while the other linked a person to the archetypal Dreamtime past. These rites imparted knowledge of the Dreamtime powers and activated catalysts of consciousness linking the Creative to the Receptive modes of perception and cognition. It was up to each individual to discover a connection to his or her ancestral totemic force: the characteristic energy form embodied in a particular place, river, or animal. The totemic traits of the koala, for example, relate both to the strength of the koala's arms, and the "silent wisdom" koala is said to possess, but be most reluctant to share.

For several years, I felt a combination of disappointment and puzzlement over the apparent absence of the koala from the cave paintings that are the primary form of documentation of the early Aboriginal culture. The appearance of the koala was also scant in any other records of rituals and other sources of tradition. It appeared that this creature was unimportant to the lives of Australia's earliest inhabitants; or perhaps there was some other explanation. I knew that koalas were abundant in many of the areas where the Aboriginal communities developed some of the most subtle and complex belief systems. I feared that the knowledge of whatever role the koalas once played now had been totally

A hungry patient in search of his lunch.

lost, since in recent decades nearly all of the Aboriginal melzigars, or tribal wise men, had died. During the same time, no young men had been initiated as they once were because of the disruption of tribal social patterns, intermarriage, and the large-scale relocation of major sectors of the Aboriginal community to urban centers in search of employment.

Over the years, and through friends at Australian universities and newspapers, as well as independent artists, I have attempted, largely without success, to move beyond the tacit barrier of secrecy surrounding the koala. Several leads uncovered in an attempt to personally meet with elders of any Aboriginal community familiar with such issues ultimately fell through. In response to both letters and telephone calls explaining my goal and connection with the Koala Hospital, I was told that I had "the right energy" and that at least basic information would be shared, but no meetings took place. Clearly, the wisdom of silence was again to win out. Communications, such as they were, did confirm what I had suspected, based on study of other mythic and initiation traditions: central symbols and, in particular, the creation of images of physical likeness, or divulgence of rituals related to the most sacred symbols, are often proscribed, even for those fully initiated members of a tradition.

The role of totems in Aboriginal lore cannot be overstated. All men, whether young souls or old souls, are linked to the ancestral past, the Dreamtime, through a totemic animal, place, or natural object. I was soon to learn that not only was Koala not to be imaged or imagined, but that few men were linked to Koala as their totem. Koala, as I was to learn, was the Universal Trickster, but unlike in so many later Western traditions, he was central to the deliverance of the Aboriginal peoples to their island continent paradise and held enormous power over the elements. Koala is Trickster, Rainmaker, and perhaps the earliest collective actualizer of the experience of the millennium. This notion of a wise and holy spirit ushering in a period of prosperity, peace, health, even wealth, is a universal archetype later to be found as a cornerstone in the construction of human religious traditions. (Some researchers have speculated that humans bond most quickly to other animals having the greatest facial likeness to themselves. Perhaps the few myths that follow, or even a pleasant afternoon spent at the zoo observing human behavior, will prove convincing.)

"Albert" by Brad Johannsen, a caricature of Albert Einstein lecturing at the Institute for Advanced Study in Princeton, New Jersey. A version of the author's complexity theorem is on the blackboard.

KOOBOR THE DROUGHT MAKER

In looking at the patterns of the world's earliest myths, one important leitmotif is surely the group often called fecundity myths. Often they are also called myths of the Great Earth Mother. Agrarian cultures, such as those of the North American Indians and Australian Aborigines, developed many such myths. Because the early Aborigines had to endure both the perils of flood as well as particularly devastating periods of drought, it should come as no surprise that the most dramatic climatic changes should be mythologically connected to one of the most sacred powers of the Dreamtime: Koala.

In one tale, an orphaned young boy named Koobor had been neglected and made to feel unwanted by his family. Among other things, they never gave him enough water. He seemed to always be thirsty.

Each morning his friends and relatives would go forage for food, leaving him behind, as he was the youngest. One day, they inadvertently forgot to hide their supply of water, which they normally did every day,

since water was in very short supply. Seeing that this would be his chance to have at least a nice drink and save up a good supply of water, Koobor found a small eucalyptus tree and hung the water buckets on its limbs.

Koobor was possessed of musical knowledge, so after hiding the buckets in the tree, he climbed into the tree and sang a special song that made the tree grow at such a pace that in practically no time it was the highest in the forest.

Eventually, those who had been out gathering food returned for the evening, panicked by having been so forgetful. It didn't take long for the group to discover Koobor high up in the tree with all of their buckets of water. They were furious and insisted that Koobor bring their water back. Koobor said that he had gone thirsty for so long and had been treated so badly that it was now their turn to go thirsty and for him to have enough to drink.

Several attempts were made by the men to catch Koobor. On at least one try, Koobor dumped a pail of water on them, knocking them to the ground. Eventually, an elder wise man climbed the tree, caught Koobor, beat him, knocked him to the ground, and called him a little thief.

As the rest of the group stood by looking in horror at the broken and battered body of Koobor, they were suddenly stunned as the body came back together, changing into a koala, which ran to a large tree and climbed to the top branches, where today he still lives and requires no water.

Koobor became entrusted with making law. Koobor's first law was that in cases of dire need, Aborigines could eat koalas, but they may not remove the skin nor break any bones until the koala was fully cooked. Should anyone decide to kill a koala, and then for any reason not obey these instructions, the Koala spirit will cause there to be such a drought that all creatures other than Koala will perish. Being a solitary fellow and not dependent upon water, he would be neither lonely nor thirsty.

Koobor the Drought Maker. It is said that if a koala is mistreated, terrible drought lasting years will result.

Most Aboriginal groups did not hunt or eat koalas. It is thought that those that did rigorously adhered to these instructions. A special reverence was always attached to the calling sounds of the koala in the night, for it was thought that should the koala ever stop singing, the trees would stop growing.

MR. KOALA AND MR. BEETLE

In another myth, following weeks of rain the hunters set out in search of food one brilliantly sunny day. Everyone except mothers with their young went on the hunt.

Mother Kangaroo moved with difficulty for her baby was at the stage when she would be evicting him from his marsupial home. She thought she should have put her son out of the pouch long before. Hearing the numerous voices of the other animals returning home to the mouth of the cave in which Mother Kangaroo was standing, she joined them and noticed that once again the sky was clouding over and looked threatening.

It was now late afternoon and rain began to fall. Fearing for the other animals, Mother Possum said, "Oh, dear me. I do hope they manage to find shelter someplace. For two weeks they have come home soaking wet."

Then a tiny squeaky voice suddenly said, "Not all of them." Everyone looked down and found Miss Mouse. Very surprised, they realized that she was right—one member of the group always came back dry as a bone and very happy, indeed: Mr. Koala!

Mrs. Goanna popped her head up and asked, "How does he do it, keep his fur so beautiful all day, despite the rains?"

"If he returns dry and beautiful with his stately gray-and-white fur today, we must all ask our husbands to try and discover his secret," said Mrs. Emu.

All agreed to this plan. As usual all the hunters returned at dusk, soaking wet. Shortly thereafter Mr. Koala arrived with his intelligent eyes and lovely dry coat, knowing full well that everyone else had returned soaking wet. Being a tease, he said, "Hmm. Everyone wet again. Well! Well!"

Angry, Mr. Kangaroo shouted, "That's enough! The next time Mr. Koala goes hunting, I will follow him, and if rain comes, I will discover how he keeps dry."

The next time was not far off. Mr. Kangaroo followed close behind, but the plan failed. Mr. Kangaroo could not help but make quite a bit of noise jumping and thumping as he does, moving through the bush. Mr.

"If the Koala should ever stop singing, the trees will stop growing."

Koala soon spotted Mr. Kangaroo and returned home. The next time, Mr. Goanna followed Mr. Koala, but he too made too much noise walking over dried sticks and leaves, for Mr. Koala had among the most sensitive ears of all the animals. Mr. Koala, suspecting that something unusual was happening, did not let Goanna know he had been spotted and led poor Goanna around in circles for hours before nonchalantly walking home.

With all attempts at learning Mr. Koala's secret failing, and because Mr. Koala spent most of the time sleeping, a secret meeting was held. Mrs. Possum called the meeting to order, stating, "We *must* find out how he does it so that we can keep dry, too!"

There were no more volunteers or suggestions, for everyone thought that Mr. Koala with his big furry ears would surely hear them. Finally, a strange voice rarely heard spoke out: "Let me try. My coloring is such that I will blend in with the trees, and I can go from tree to tree without making a sound."

The group laughed. Could such a mode of travel exist? The group gazed down at Mr. Beetle, whom they had always regarded as totally useless and insignificant. Suddenly, Mr. Beetle jumped and landed on a leaf near Mr. Kangaroo's ear and whispered, "Please let me try. I know what you think of me. Maybe if I can finally do something the rest of you can't, you'll finally accept me."

Mr. Goanna overheard this conversation and brought the group to order. Mr. Kangaroo spoke: "It is true that Mr. Beetle is very small, but he can fly in silence and has as much right as the rest of us to prove his worth."

The next time the rains came, Mr. Koala set out with Mr. Beetle following along. Mr. Koala was now on the lookout for followers but saw no one. As the rain once again came, he climbed a tall gum tree and broke off two small twigs from the highest branch. Holding one in each hand, he began to sing to the clouds. By now, Mr. Beetle was safely hidden under the bark of a nearby gum tree, absolutely stunned. It had never occurred to Mr. Beetle, or any of the others, that Mr. Koala was, in fact, the all-knowing cosmic spirit Gundir. Mr. Beetle hung on to the tree spellbound, listening to the loud roar Mr. Koala was capable of making. Mr. Beetle didn't dare move or breathe.

As Mr. Koala waved his sticks and sang, he activated the powers of

An encounter between Mr.
Koala and Mr. Beetle,
according to legend.

Gundir. The rain clouds parted and quickly moved away, leaving the tree dry as the sunlight shone down on Mr. Koala. For Mr. Beetle, this was quite an experience. He was definitely shaken, as he made his way home. The next day he told the others what he had witnessed. All of the others, including Mr. Koala, just laughed at him, telling such an astonishing and obviously contrived tale. "Imagine such a power among us," they protested. Infuriated, Mr. Beetle decided that he would teach the others the special song that he had heard Mr. Koala sing. This didn't please Mr. Koala in the least.

His pleasant smile was suddenly replaced with the rather surly face that he often maintains to this day. From that moment on, Mr. Koala decided to sit still pretending not to hear a thing and maintain the cynical expression which he often bears today.

The koala is known by many different names within different aboriginal languages, including *banjora, boorbee, burendong, carbora, coolabun, koala, koob-bor, kulla, kurbo-roo, nargoon, nurrumpi, wirngill, and yarri.*

The koala, according to legend, is the only animal who pretends not to hear. Every other animal upon hearing an odd sound will react in some way. Some become more still in order to listen more keenly. Others will move their ears, some react with flight, some scurry and hide. Mr. Koala sits quietly and unperturbed with a surly expression on his face, pretending not to hear. But do not be deceived into forgetting Mr. Koala's great disguise.

KOALA AND THE RAINBOW

Another myth of importance deals with the symbol of the rainbow. The myth is important, since it appears among several Aboriginal groups in slightly different forms. In addition, it is a creation myth of the "Tree People," those totemic spirits living in the trees: Koala, Possum, and Flying Fox, a large bat.

In the very beginning, the earth was all land. This did not last for long as lengthy periods of rain ensued, creating the rivers, creeks, and eventually the oceans. As water levels increased, the animals and men became increasingly cut off from the others by the growing lakes, rivers, and oceans.

A series of islands was formed as the water rose, far from what is now known as Australia. The men who lived on one of these islands were all very skilled at throwing boomerangs. Tales were commonplace of their ability to throw the boomerangs and intercept birds in flight and of their ability to throw them so far as to totally disappear from sight before returning. The people on this island were competitive, having frequent contests of skill. One man was particularly known for both his lack of modesty and his prowess. He often claimed that he could throw his boomerang to any place in the islands, including the most distant one, and back. One of the many who doubted his claim countered one day saying, "How would anyone know if you had succeeded, if you throw your boomerang so far?" Strong Man replied, "The answer is simple. What happens to boomerangs when they are thrown?" "They come back to the thrower," his detractor replied. "What happens if it hits a tree or something?" "It stays there, falling to the ground," the critic once again replied. "Then," said Strong Man, "the question is answered. If I throw my boomerang to the farthest island and it doesn't return, then everyone will know that I succeeded." Strong Man's inquisitor observed that there was little point in talking of such things without having done them and challenged Strong Man to the test.

Strong Man studied his collection of boomerangs in detail and picked several up, stroking them, attempting to balance them between his two middle fingers. Finally, after whirling the selected boomerang faster and faster over his head, he let it fly. It departed so quickly that only a few spectators could catch sight of it as it sped out over the ocean. Even the skeptical one would have to say that it was possible it had landed on a distant island. True to his nature, though, he called the group's attention to the obvious alternative: The boomerang might have fallen into the sea and never made it to its final destination.

Strong Man was annoyed, proclaiming that this could not happen, but if it had, it still would have returned, cutting its way through the sea, if necessary. Holding fast, the skeptic asserted that the only way they were ever going to truly be able to verify the claim would be to go to the distant island themselves.

While this seemed an impractical idea, a small boy said, "I know how to do it." The doubting one, an older man, said, "Shut up. We hear too much from you all the time. You would be well off to eat your food as the other children do. I have seen how you refuse to eat properly, spitting food out all the time!"

"That's because nobody has ever brought me a koala to eat; I like them best," the young boy said.

"How do you know what your favorite is if you have never eaten one?" the older man argued.

"How do you know that there is an island where the boomerang landed, far out to sea, if you have never seen it?"

"Because several born before I was have spoken of it," the older man said, becoming visibly annoyed with the tenacity of the young boy.

The boy said, "Then in all likelihood they ate koala meat, too. My sister's brother caught a koala this morning. It's over there by that tree." The old man, wishing to be rid of this amazing child, picked up the body of the koala and threw it at the boy, knocking him over. The boy then took the body of the koala off to the beach where he thought he might try cooking it. As he made the first incision, the intestines fell out, but immediately inflated, forming a magnificent multicolored shiny arch into the sky, over the sea, with the distant end so far away that it was impossible to see it.

The old man appeared on the beach, undoubtedly having seen the colorful arch in the sky. "What have you done?" he asked. "If you wish to taste koala meat, have your mother cook it for you."

"No. Now I want to see what Koala has done. I think we can go and find the boomerang, as Koala has built us a beautiful bridge," said the young boy's brother-in-law, who, along with many others, had now assembled on the beach, seeing the magnificent colors of the arch. He put his foot on the sparkling bridge and was followed by the boy, his mother, father, great uncle, aunts, sisters, and, finally, his brothers.

The crossing was not easy. The arch built by Koala was so high that it subjected the travelers to intense heat from the sun. There was, of course, neither water nor food. Eventually, they came to the end of the bridge, sliding along the down side. When they reached the land at the bottom of the arch, they were stunned. Never had they imagined such a place so much greener than their own land. Lush forests of gum trees were everywhere. There was sparkling water clearer than anything they had ever seen, making it possible to observe fantastic forms of sea life and corals. The new land had cloud formations above it unlike anything they had experienced, forming faces and landscapes. As they watched, the rainbow arch slowly disappeared as the sun grew brighter and a symphony of birds began to play.

Suddenly a complete silence came over the group as all in the party were gawking at the little boy who had wished to taste koala meat: He had turned into a magnificent koala with a rich coat and big fluffy ears! His brother-in-law had been turned into a cat! The group was ecstatic and set out to explore their new home, and forever was thankful to the spirit of Koala for providing the way to the Island Continent, and vowed never to eat or kill Koala.

GETTING TO KNOW YOUR TOTEMIC ANIMAL SPIRIT

IN ORDER TO experience the unique connectedness one may have with one's totem, it is necessary to have at least an intuitive understanding of how the universe operates, according to the Aboriginal conception of it. Interestingly, many of the basic conceptions prefigure ideas that now, thousands of years later, are coming to be accepted through the metaphors of physics and psychology. Indeed, models of inner space (psychology and subatomic physics) often mirror models of outer space (astronomy and cosmology).

At the risk of doing great injury to one of the oldest and most important early sets of human tradition and myth, it is useful to set forth a few basic ideas. Many of these ideas may seem vague or illusive and difficult to grasp. Rather than to try to understand them, focus on the tone of what is being described, as these are ideas of process rather than content.

According to Aboriginal thought, the earth as we know it formed from a source of energy called Baiame. Though Baiame was nonphysical in terms of our universe, it was responsible for energy taking on the basic expressions of light, heat, chemical energy, and what today are referred to as magnetism and electricity. All life began in response to the power of images held by Baiame. Collective experience is cumulative and is added to the Yowie, or life-form energy, evolving and enlarging as new experiences, over thousands of years, occur. There is Yowie energy at different levels of development in all life forms.

All around us is the Dowie, a resistanceless intangible ether that indefinitely retains all interactions with it—forever. The Dowie is inhabited or possessed by all life forms, yet it has no location, since it is simultaneously invisible and ubiquitous. Changes in the Dowie occur at velocities greater than the speed of light.

Because the Yowie, or subtle essence that evolves with life forms, changes at a pace so different from the Dowie, the two realms are buffered from one another by a protective layer called the Mullowill. This protective bubble is said to envelop all living beings. Injury to the Mullowill, according to Aboriginal teaching, can lead to mental illness and even death. Should this layer become too thin or penetrable, intense forces from the Dowie implode, causing sickness. Should Mullowill become too impenetrable, one's spirit ceases to have contact with the universe and becomes quite literally a lost soul.

While normal people have little contact with the Dowie, shamans, healers, and wise men have regular contact with the Dowie and are not overwhelmed by it. The average person may have, in his or her lifetime, a few momentary experiences when contents of the Dowie or collective powers spill over into personal experience, the Yowie. Today, we would most often label these experiences as intuitions or hunches. Of course, the most frequently encountered realm of the Dowie experience is dreaming. The notion of either a spiritual or psychological component of

Koala is a sacred totem thousands of years old, yet for many its meaning is locked within the silence of a waning oral tradition.

According to Aboriginal lore, the Dowie is a universal energy with which all life forms interact. Since the beginning of time, koalas have been protected by the Dowie.

any life form not working toward the best interests of that being is nowhere to be found in the Aboriginal conception of the universe.

Initiation plays a critical role on both a collective, societal, and individual, psychological level. The Universal laws are shared with an Aboriginal youth at the time of initiation. He knows that Baiame, the life force or energy, took the form of a man and convened the first Bora, or organized social meeting, where the laws of the universe were presented. To this day, the first Bora forms the basis for one of the most important ceremonies and calls for the enactment of special abilities uniquely held by each member of the community. These capacities, different in every living being, play into enabling different roles within ceremonial customs and magic, such as Rainmaking. They also are directly related to powers one has inherited ancestrally. These may otherwise be embodied in sacred spaces, ancestral animals, or mythic figures. Once initiated, one presumably has the ability to call upon these powers or spiritual forces, yet one never calls upon such a force one is not intimately familiar with.

The effect produced by interaction with one's ancestral or totemic energy source depends upon the interplay of the Dowie forces. These energies are thought to be effective only when operating in harmony with one's subtle or ancient ancestors. If it was not the case that all living

You cannot acquire your own totemic spirit; like Koala, it "acquires" you!

things are vibrationally linked to all that came before them, then totems would be of little importance. Since in the Aboriginal conception, there is a collective link between each individual and the past of all other animals and inanimate things of antiquity, the ongoing effectiveness of Baiame is related to the degree of harmony found among all living beings and objects. For this reason, self-knowledge takes on very great importance. Since we are all the product of our collective pasts, knowledge of our totem is a very important element of self-knowledge.

Modern humans, to the extent that they are at all receptive to these ideas, usually ask, "How does one acquire one's totem?" In fact, your totem acquires you. When one encounters one's totem, it will make itself known at the appropriate time. There is an intense interchange of energy and feeling between each person and his or her totem. Once found, within Aboriginal lore, such an event is to be celebrated and cherished. One must from then on devote oneself to protecting and caring for that totem in some real way. Dreams are important signposts capable of signifying one's totemic connections. They should not be viewed as dark wish fulfillments of some negative side of the personality. Rather, Aboriginal teaching on the subject of dreams counsels a far more delicate approach, looking at dreams as signals of elements of one's self, or environment, that might be neglected at that point in one's life. Events of importance may be presaged in dreams as well, of course, as encounters with one's totem.

In the case of animal totems, or animism, the participants begin responding with an energy that suggests much more than instructive behavior. Energies of the Dowie are activated, causing collective forces to take over. One might think that such a powerful experience could be overwhelming or even terrifying for an individual. This turns out not to be so, since in order for the individual to be sensitive enough to perceive what is happening, he or she would have to have already gone through so many personal trials, initiation experiences, and possibly ecstatic experiences that such things would no longer be frightening or threatening in any personal sense of the word. It is therefore said that one's totem "knows" if one is ready to be acquired.

Koala as totem is a sacred subject about which few living men know, and fewer will discuss. The myths described earlier, while hundreds if not thousands of years old, were passed along with dozens of other oral traditions and were not widespread, coming from only a few localities. Because Koala is such an important figure in the Aboriginal pantheon, it is ironic that its image and meaning were so tightly held and not widely disseminated. Yet again this is a pattern seen in many mythic traditions around the globe. When looking at the patterns of meaning that are attached to totems in different cultures throughout the world, patterns, not surprisingly, slowly begin to appear much as an image begins to form on a piece of photographic paper submerged in developing chemicals.

While I studied collections of Australian Aboriginal legends, and listening to both scholars and the children of those who knew firsthand, faint images of patterns, or what Carl Jung called "archetypes," began to emerge. I have found it important to bear in mind that the finest instructors in these matters have been the koalas themselves, with their ever so subtle behaviors. It would seem that the older the totemic figure is, the more subtle its "personality." For this reason, it requires great sensitivity, something the aboriginal wise men definitely had, to understand and feel each koala's distinctly different personality.

Sometimes Koala acts like a so-called Senex figure: the wise old man carrying a lamp in the darkness of night and often represented in Western mythology by Chronos. At other times, Koala is far more like the Trickster, one of the more complex figures in the pantheon of archetypal beings. Indeed this "trickster" side of Koala is easily observed in a couple of the myths we have just seen.

Though much could be said here about dreams of animals and other totems, I maintain that the traditional Western psychological interpretation of animals appearing symbolically in dreams, representing the untamed, bestial, sexual side of the personality, is largely incorrect and more a symptom of the pervasive cultural effect of religions far less mature and subtle than the traditions of which these symbols were first a part. The role of animals, including humans, in nature are mutually interdependent; we all need each other for the overall ecosystem to work. The same was true in the Chinese, Roman, and Greek systems of mythology, where the gods needed each other, as well. It is not a coincidence that many of the gods were represented in animal forms. In dream work with my clients (the human ones) my approach was formatively instructed by a dream I had after my first visit to Port Macquarie and the Koala Hospital.

In myth, Koala played a
central role in maintaining
natural law.

Despite his playful
appearance, Koala is believed
to be the embodiment of the
Wise Old Man, possessor of
timeless secrets.

For thousands of years,
Koala was recognized as the
Trickster in the Trees. If
abused, he would steal the
water and create drought.

Near the hospital is a magnificent piece of land that extends out into the Tasman Sea. At the tip of the land is a beautiful white lighthouse. Though it is very windy most of the time there, I often drive to this point and am carried away by the sound of the rough sea bashing against the large boulders far below the lighthouse and the feeling of the wind gusts against my face and hair. Standing there constellates the feeling of being literally at the end of the world. The night after my first discovery of this magic lookout, I dreamed that I was there on a moonless misty night and that the lighthouse was a huge koala. One intensely white beacon of light, blinding in strength if one looked directly into it, originated from each eye, cutting a perfectly straight path miles long out to sea, providing the way for lost souls.

It is now clear to me that such animal totem dreams, as with other types, have a far more significant and transpersonal meaning than ever understood by the major schools of Western psychology. The animals are there to help us see in the dark—our darkness. The elements of one's totem correspond to the those elements we need in order to see into our own darkness: not a threatening, horror-laden darkness, but rather the darkness of the night—of eternal return.

Another important way to look at totems is as part of the collective human experience. As Senex, or Wise Old Man, Koala was seen as a possessor of secrets. As such, Koala is timeless. He is the collective reservoir of endless experiences, yet typically the Senex figure is not anxious to dispense with his wisdom; indeed, he need not be in any hurry. Often the most effective way to learn the secrets of the Wise Man is simply to spend quiet time with him, carefully observing his ways, much as Mr. Beetle did in the myth. As related in the myths we have seen, Koala is not only Wise Man but played an important role in delivering Australia's native people to their permanent home, controlling the climate, and in promulgating natural law.

The other and perhaps more interesting universal form prefigured by Koala is the Trickster. Here we again find a parallel to the North American Indian tradition, particularly the cycle of stories within the traditions of the Winnebago Indians. Of particular note, aside from the Trickster's fondness for pranks and games of deception, is his fundamentally dual nature as half animal and half god. The Trickster is totally adept at changing his shape and form and can do so in the service of healing.

Aboriginal lore speaks of Koala as a healer and guide for lost souls, much as the beacon of this lighthouse near the Koala Hospital guides ships lost at sea.

Among many other things, he is truly the first "wounded healer." With the exception of the origin of the myth of Kur-bo-roo, I have been unable to locate any Aboriginal myths in which Koala appears as a great healer. This is clearly one of the major roles of the Trickster, based upon later evolution of the myth. Trickster is a great healer in part because of his powers of empathy, stemming from his own suffering.

As Jung pointed out in his important philosophical studies of myth, the Trickster is "an archetypal psychic structure of extreme antiquity" and is a symbolic form of "undifferentiated human consciousness, corresponding to a psyche that has hardly left the animal world." Although the Trickster is quite capable of healing, changing forms, and pulling off nasty pranks of all sorts, he has an unending eagerness to learn and to this day exerts an enormous degree of collective influence through those who are the front runners of the collective psyche: the artists, musicians, healers, inventors, and other visionaries.

WHAT THE FUTURE HOLDS

Perhaps the most popular children's tales in Australia are the adventures and misadventures of Blinky Bill, a naughty little koala. Hero of a beautiful set of stories conceived by Dorothy Wahl, Blinky Bill has been further popularized by John Williamson's prescient song "Goodbye Blinky Bill."

While the story of the Koala Hospital told in this book chronicles the selfless efforts of some of the residents of a town that was home to hundreds if not thousands of koalas long before the first hospital house was built, the outlook for the survival of the koala is bleak. With the continued destruction of its habitat, even if present disease factors were to be eliminated from the equation, in roughly ten years' time, there will simply be neither home nor food for the koala. Trees must be planted and the destruction of forests containing the koalas' eucalyptus leaves halted.

Even as this book was being written, massive fires were consuming hundreds of thousands of acres of trees and wildlife in New South Wales. Though the popular press reported that hundreds of homes had been destroyed in the wealthier suburbs of Sydney, virtually no mention was made of the fact that while the owners of these abodes probably have insurance to enable them to reconstruct their homes, many more thou-

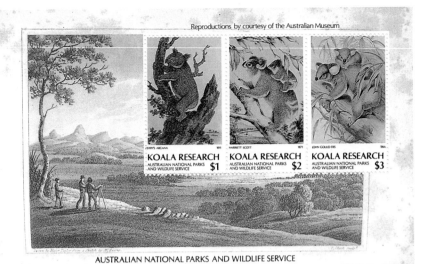

KOALA RESEARCH

1988-89

Current efforts to save the koala focus on education and research, a cause aided by the sale of these attractive stamps from the Australian National Parks and Wildlife Service.

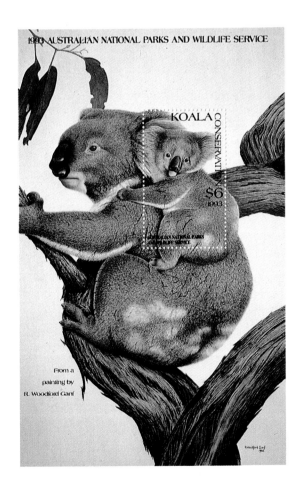

The popular song "Goodbye Blinky Bill" by John Williamson is a plea for efforts to help save the koala. © E MUSIC PTY., LTD. Printed with the kind permission of E MUSIC PTY., LTD., Australia.

KOALA KOALA

JOHN WILLIAMSON

Koala Koala—We love you
But we chop down your home
and you run.

Koala Koala—where do you go
when we take your gum tree away.

Please don't run on the road
and please don't cry.
Help is on its way
We're gonna learn what makes you die
Gonna send in some money today.

Koala Koala

You can't dig a hole
or live in a roof
or hang from a big fig tree.
If I plant you a special Eucalypt
Will you come and live with me?

Koalas they used to be everywhere
What a paradise it could be.
A walk in the bush would be heaven
Bring the Dreamtime back to me.

sands of Australians have lost their lives in these conflagrations, not to mention their magnificent green forested dwellings. These fires, reported to be the worst in the 200 years since Australia was settled by whites, are now known to have been in large measure set by human arsonists.

While the region served by the Koala Hospital is not at risk at present, volunteers from other areas of New South Wales, who have received training at the hospital and who have released rehabilitated koalas into the wild, have now seen many of those territories destroyed by fire. Is there no insurance policy for the koala and the many other ancient and beautiful cohabitants of this planet who are the bearers of the Dreamtime against our darker side?

I end this book as it began, by noting that one of the planet's oldest and wisest inhabitants is about to disappear unless aggressive action is taken to protect the koala's habitat. At the start of this century, new settlers killed over two million koalas for their fur. At the end of this century, let us right this terrible wrong by ensuring the continued survival of this very special Earth Spirit. When the last member of a species disappears, so, too, does a part of the earth and a part of each of us. As Beebe pointed out, "an entire heaven and an entire earth must pass before such a one can be again."

To contribute to the effort to save the koalas or obtain further information about koalas, my work, or the Koala Preservation Society, please write or telephone the address and telephone number below. Also, please know that every penny goes toward the effort to protect, heal, and ensure a future for the koala and its habitat.

Ken Phillips
Koala Preservation Society
P.O. Box 612, Cooper Station
New York, N.Y. 10003
1-800-989-KOALA (5625)
from outside U.S.A.: 212-477-4370

1994
KOALA CONSERVATION

AUSTRALIAN NATURE CONSERVATION AGENCY

$8

FROM A PAINTING BY DANIEL SMITH

KOALA CONSERVATION

AUSTRALIAN NATURE
CONSERVATION AGENCY

The latest koala conservation stamp from the Australian Nature Conservation Agency. The koala's future is in our hands.

149

BIBLIOGRAPHY

Australian Koala Foundation, Queensland National Parks and Wildlife Service, eds. "Koala Management." In Austr. Koala Found. Conf. on Koala Management in Currumbin/Brisbane, Qld. Australia, Number 123,

Barrett, Charles. *The Australian Animal Book*. Melbourne, Australia: Oxford Univ. Press, 1943.

Bergin, T.J. "The Koala." In *Taronga Symposium on Koala Biology, Management and Medicine in Sydney, Australia*. Edited by T.J. Bergin. Zoological Parks Board of NSW, 239,

Buchanan, Harry. *Gumbaynggir Dreamings*—I. English Pilot Edition ed. Edited by Gumbaynggir Language & Culture Group. Lismore, NSW, Australia: Gumbaynggir Language & Culture Group, 1992.

Burnet, Noel. *The Blue Gum Family at Koala Park*. Sydney, Australia: W.A. Pepperday & Co., 1932.

Burt, Denise. *Birth of a Koala*. Davis, CA: Australian Book Service, 1988.

———. *I Am Not a Bear*. Ashburton, Vic. Australia: Buttercup Books Pty., 1985.

Cairns, Sylvia. *Uncle Willie Mackenzie's Legends of the Goundirs*. Sydney, Australia: Jacaranda Press.

Cowan, James. *The Elements of the Aboriginal Tradition*. Longmead, Shaftsbury, Dorset, England: Element Books, Ltd., 1992.

———. *Letters from a Wild State*. Earth Quest, Longmead, Shaftsbury, Dorset, England: Element Books, Ltd., 1991.

———. *Mysteries of the Dreamtime*. Dorset, England: Prism Press, 1989.

Cronin, Leonard, ed. *Koala: Australia's Endearing Marsupial*. Frenchs Forest, NSW, Australia: Reed Books Pty., Ltd., 1987.

Eberhard, I.H. "Ecology of the Koala." Univ. of Adelaide Press, 1972.

Ellis, Jean, A. *From the Dreamtime*. North Blackburn, Vic., Australia: Collins Dove, 1991.

Gardner, Robert L. *The Rainbow Serpent: Studies in Jungian Psychology by Jungian Analysts*. Toronto: Inner City Books, 1990.

Grzimek, Bernhard, ed. *Grzimek's Animal Life Encyclopedia*. Vol. 1. New York: Van Nostrand Reinhold Co., 1982.

Havecker, Cyril. *Understanding Aboriginal Culture.* Sydney, Australia: Cosmos Periodicals Pty., Ltd., 1987.

Judge, Joseph. "Child of Gonwana." *National Geographic.* February 1988, 170–177.

Lawlor, John. *Voices of the First Day.* Rochester, VT: Inner Traditions, 1991.

Lee, Anthony, and Roger Martin. *The Koala: A Natural History.* From *Australian Natural History Series,* edited by Simon Ward III. Kensington, NSW, Australia: New South Wales Univ. Press, 1988.

Lee, A.K., K.A. Handasyde, and G.D. Sanson, eds. *Biology of the Koala.* Chipping Norton, NSW, Australia: Surrey Beatty & Sons Pty., Ltd., 1990.

Lee, Tony. "Koalas." *Australian Geographic.* July 1991, 50–66.

Lewis, F. "Rehabilitation of the Koala in Victoria." *Victorian Naturalist* 70 (March 1954): 199–206.

Macdonald, David. *Encyclopedia of Mammals.* edited by Peter Forbes. New York: Facts On File, 1984.

Massaolo, Aldo. *Bunjil's Cave.* Lansdowne, Melbourne, Australia: 1968.

Matthews, Rupert. *Koalas.* Colourful Australia, Godalming, Surrey, England: Colour Library Books, Ltd., 1991.

Morcombe, Michael. *Australian Marsupials and other Native Animals.* Dee Why West, NSW, Australia: Summit Books, 1972.

Mountford, Charles P. *Aboriginal Conception Beliefs.* Melbourne, Australia: Hyland House, 1977.

Norledge, Mildred. *Aboriginal Legends from Eastern Australia.* Sydney, Australia: A.H. & A.W. Reed Pty., 1968.

Norst, Marlene. *Ferdinand Bauer.* Art in Natural History, London: British Museum (Natural History), 1989.

Nowak, Ronald M., ed. *Walker's Mammals of the World.* 5th ed., Vol. 1. Baltimore, MD: Johns Hopkins Univ. Press, 1991.

NSW, Koala Preservation Society. *The Koala.* Monograph by Koala Preservation Soc. of NSW, 1987.

Phillips, Bill. *Koalas: The Little Australians We'd All Hate to Lose.* Canberra, Act., Australia: Australian Govt. Publishing Service, 1990.

Phillips, Ken. "This Wise Old Trickster Is Not a Bear." *The New York Times,* June 5, 1991, A 28.

Power, Phyllis. *Legends from the Outback.* London, England: J.M. Demb & Sons, Ltd., 1958.

Pyne, Stephen J. *Burning Bush.* New York: Henry Holt & Co., 1991.

Reed, A.W. *Aboriginal Fables.* Frenchs Forest, NSW, Australia: Reed Books Pty., Ltd., 1978.

———. *Aboriginal Legends.* Balgolaw, NSW, Australia: Reed Books Pty., Ltd., 1978.

———. *Aboriginal Words.* Frenchs Forest, NSW, Australia: Reed Books Pty., Ltd., 1965.

Serventy, Vincent. *Koalas.* Australian Nature Series, Frenchs Forest, NSW, Australia: Child & Assoc., 1989.

Smith, Ramsay. *Myths & Legends of the Australian Aboriginals.* New York: Farrar & Rinehart,

Thomas, W.J. *Some Myths and Legends of the Australian Aborigines.* Melbourne, Australia: Whitcomb & Tombs, 1943.

INDEX

Aborigines, xiv, 28, 38, 116
Aboriginal beliefs, 116–142
Agrarian cultures, 123
Annual cycles, 53
Antibiotics, 102
Arboreals, 37
Archetypes, 139
Australia Koala Foundation, 10, 13

Baiame, 135–136
Bandicoots, 4
Bauer, Ferdinand, 14–15
Bears, 2
Beebe, William, xi
Behavior, 54, 57, 58
Bellowing, 50, 52, 54
Boomerangs, 131
Bora, 136
British colonialization, 120
Bush fires, 95

Caecum, 27
Canfield, Paul, 45
Capillary action, 20
Captivity, 109
Cave paintings, 120
Cheek pouch, 33
Chlamydia, 47–49

Chronos, 139
Coat, 11
Cockram, Frank, 69
Collective past, 138
Colon, 34
Conjunctivitis, 44, 47
Continental Drift, 21
Corridors, 41
Cosmogony, 118
Creation myths, 116, 120
Creation of images, 122
Cubby, 69

Death, causes of, 44–48
Diet, 27
Digestion, 31–36
Diprotodonta, 5
Discovery, 11
Disease, 36–37
DNA, 29
Dogs, 88
Dowie, 135, 137, 138
Dreaming, 63, 135, 138, 139
Dreamtime, 38, 116, 120, 122

Ear tags, 51, 91
Earth Mother, 123
Einstein, Albert, 123

Ellis, Jean A., 116
Esophagus, 33
Eucalyptus, 7–9, 18, 27–29
Eucalyptus oil, 28

Faison, Jim, 109
Family life, 23–27
Fecundity myths, 123
Feet, 7
Fiber, 28, 29
Fires, 97–100, 144, 147
Food trees, 8
Fossils, 21, 37
Fripp, Karen, 102
Fur, 16
Fur, trade, 12
Further information, 148

Gestation, 11
Gestation period, 5
"Goodbye Blinky Bill," xv, 72, 144, 146
Gundir, 128
Gunyah, 75, 93

Habitat loss, 22, 40, 41, 144, 148
Hairline, 78
Hearing, 130
Hoover, Herbert, 12
Hospital (Koala), v, 36–38, 66–115
Hunting, 12

Ileum, 33, 34
Infection, 103
Initiation, 120, 136, 138
Injuries, by traffic, 38–40
Intuitions, 135
Island Continent, 133

Jackson, Alan, 69
Jung, Carl, 139, 143

Kangaroos, 6
"Koala, Koala," 147
Koala Preservation Society of New South
    Wales, 10, 66, 72, 94, 148
Koobor, 123–125

Laurasia, 21
Leaf content, 28, 29
Legislation, 12
Life span, 11

Mackensie, W. C., 34
Marsupial, 2–7
Mating call, 50, 52
Mating season, 49
Mayo, Will, 44
Milk, 24
Mr. Beetle, 126–129
Mullowill, 135
Multiorgan disease, 48

National Parks and Wildlife Service
    (AUS.), 10, 72, 75
Nutrients, 28

Opposable thumbs, 7
Oral traditions, 118
Oxley Electric Company, 97, 98, 103

Pangea, 21
Pap, 32
Pebbles, 79–81, 94
Phenols, 30
Phrastolarctos cinereas, 6
Physiology, 20
Placenta, 4
Pneumonia, 47
Polar ice caps, 21
Pop Eye, 69

Port Macquarie, 66, 68
Port Macquarie News, 69, 71
Postures, 56
Pouch, 4
Predator, 11
Protein, 29
Psychology (koala), 60–65
  depression, 106
  dreaming, 63
  human bonding, 65, 122
  personality, 65, 82
  play, 63
  role of father, 61
  surrogate mother, 60
  tooling behavior, 63

Queensland koalas, 7

Rainmaker, 122, 137
Rainbow, 131–133
Release, 112
Roto House, 71, 87

Satellite imaging, 13
Senex figure, 139, 142
Sex, 49
Sexual behavior, 58
Shamans, 135
Size, 11
Sleep, 28, 82, 83
Stamps, 145, 149
Sternal gland, 55, 57
"Strong Man," 131
Stress, 2, 41, 44

Strom, Allen, 12
Subdural hematoma, 94
Subspecies, 11
Sun Herald Koala Fund, 75
Surrogate mother, 60
Swimming pool deaths, 89

Tasman Sea, 88, 142
Temperature regulation, 16–20
Tannin, 30
Teeth, 32
Territoriality, 57
Territorial marking, 58
Terry Glen, 95–115
Tiny Tim, 70
Totemic forces, 120
Totems, 122, 133, 138
Tree People, 131
Tree planting, 68
Trickster, 122, 130, 139, 141, 142, 143

University of Sydney, 94
Uptin, Charles, 68

Wahl, Dorothy, 144
Water intake, 7
Water storage, 35
Weight, 11
Williamson, John, xv, 72, 144, 147
Wise Old Man, 140, 142

Yowie, 135